Editing Wor.

Editing Women is a collection of original essays by six women contributors, representing various disciplines, dealing with texts that range
from the medieval to the modern. Questions regarding the role of
gender, the exercise of power in the process of editing texts by women,
cultural contexts and constraints of the author's time, and the suppression and revision of material after the death of the author are
among the problems addressed by scholars who are only too aware of
the editorial control they themselves exercise.

ANN M. HUTCHISON is Visiting Professor at the Pontifical Institute of
Mediaeval Studies, Toronto.

Editing Women

Edited by Ann M. Hutchison

UNIVERSITY OF WALES PRESS
Cardiff 1998

© University of Toronto Press Incorporated 1998
Toronto Buffalo
Printed in Canada

Printed on acid-free paper

First published in Great
Britain in 1998 by
University of Wales Press,
6 Gwennyth Street,
Cathays, Cardiff
CF2 4YD

British Library Cataloguing in Publication Data

A catalogue record for this book is available from
the British Library.

ISBN 0-7083-1459-7

Contents

Notes on Contributors

NAOMI BLACK, Professor Emerita of Political Science at York University, has published articles on women's organizations and feminist theory as well as *Social Feminism* (1989) and *Canadian Women: A History* (co-author, 1988 and 1996). She is currently editing Virginia Woolf's *Three Guineas* for Blackwell's Shakespeare Head edition of the works of Virginia Woolf.

JOAN COLDWELL, Professor of English and founding Director of the Women's Studies Programme at McMaster University, has worked for a number of years on the poetry and prose of Anne Wilkinson and has published her journals and autobiography in *The Tightrope Walker: Autobiographical Writings of Anne Wilkinson* (1992).

MARGARET ANNE DOODY is Andrew W. Mellon Professor of Humanities and English and Director of the Comparative Literature Program at Vanderbilt University. She has edited some of the works of Frances Burney and Jane Austen, and has written a literary biography of Frances Burney, *The Life in the Works* (1988). Her latest book, *The True Story of the Novel* (1996), a finalist for the National Book Critics' Circle Award, has been widely reviewed in the United States and England. In addition to her scholarly work, she has published some fiction, most notably *Aristotle Detective*, a book which has appeared in several editions and been translated into French and German.

GERMAINE GREER is a fellow of Newnham College, Cambridge. *Kissing the Rod: An Anthology of Seventeenth-Century Verse* (1988) displays her long-standing interest in the writings of seventeenth-century women. She is currently engaged in recovering the works of the royalist poet, Katherine Philips, and has been publishing the results at the Stump Cross Press, of which she is founder. Her most recent book, the provocative study entitled *Slip-Shod Sibyls: Recognition, Rejection and the Woman Poet*, appeared in 1995.

ISOBEL GRUNDY, Henry Marshall Tory Professor in the Department of English at the University of Alberta in Edmonton, has achieved an international reputation for her work on Lady Mary Wortley Montagu. Her recent publications include an edition of Montagu's *Romance Writings* (1996) and *Selected Letters* (1997). She has played a major role in the rediscovery of women writers in English and currently, as co-investigator of the Orlando Project, is engaged in producing a history of women's writing in the British Isles. In 1997 she was elected a Fellow of the Royal Society of Canada.

FELICITY RIDDY, Professor of English and Director of the Centre for Medieval Studies at the University of York in England, is a leading scholar in the field of Middle English and Scots language and literature. She publishes in the fields of Arthurian literature, romance, gender studies, and urban culture, and lately has paid particular attention to writing by and about medieval women.

ANN M. HUTCHISON, Visiting Professor at the Pontifical Institute of Mediaeval Studies, teaches medieval literature and is also interested in women's education and female spirituality in the later Middle Ages. Her research centres on St Birgitta of Sweden and the Bridgettine Order, in particular its only English house, Syon Abbey.

Acknowledgments

The annual Conference on Editorial Problems is a result of the collective effort of the conference committee and I would like to thank committee members of the past two years for their encouragement and support. In particular, I am grateful to Roberta Frank, who not only nominated me to the committee, making it possible to organize a conference on women writers, but who also was on hand and generous with support, encouragement, and effective counsel. I would like to thank G.E. (Jerry) Bentley, who as chair worked on my behalf to facilitate the conference; Donald Moggridge, treasurer, who assisted in the initial planning stages; and very especially John Grant, who stepped in as acting treasurer (when Don went on sabbatical) and skillfully handled the nuts and bolts of our finances. Fred Unwalla created the elegant publicity and programmes and assisted in many other important ways behind the scenes, as did Jennifer Forbes, whose administrative and interpersonal skills facilitated the planning and averted many potential disasters. I am extremely grateful to them both for their contribution in making the conference the great success it was. I would also like to thank the students, Katerina Atanassova, Anita Boldt, Alison Booth, Michael Cichon, Eric Graff, Steven Killings, Jason Nolan, Tamara O'Callaghan, Beverley Rapp, and Amanda Spencer, who assisted with registration, social events, and audio-visual equipment, and James Carley, who gave up part of his research leave to be on hand to help.

For their financial support, I am grateful to the Social Sciences and Humanities Research Council, whose grant allowed the conference to become a reality, to the British Council in Canada, and to the University of Toronto, which through the assistance of the following groups made the conference memorable: the Office of the Provost, the School of Graduate Studies, the Faculty of Arts and Science, the Centre for

Medieval Studies, the Pontifical Institute of Mediaeval Studies, the Departments of English, History, and Women's Studies, the Graduate Collaborative Programme in Women's Studies, and the University of Toronto Press. University College and the University College Alumni Association provided major support; we value their continuing interest in our annual conferences.

I am especially grateful to those who chaired each session: Linda Hutcheon, Ann B. Shteir, Heather Jackson, Lorna Marsden, Bonnie Wheeler, and Heather Murray. I would also like to thank the President of the University of Toronto, J. Robert S. Prichard, for opening the conference, and the Principal of University College, Lynd Forguson, for his welcome to the College. My special thanks to Marie Korey, librarian of Massey College, who prepared an exhibition of a number of the editions under discussion, and to Robert Brandeis, librarian of Victoria College, who loaned much of the material. For assistance with the publication of the papers, I am deeply indebted to the wisdom and experience of Fred Unwalla, and I would also like to thank Michael Kulikowski for his able copy editing and checking. I am grateful to Gwen Peroni for her careful and elegant typesetting. Suzanne Rancourt, Kristen Pederson, and Barbara Porter at the University of Toronto Press have been encouraging and always helpful. Finally, I would like to thank the six speakers for papers that raised important issues and, indeed, continue to generate discussion.

ANN M. HUTCHISON

Introduction

The 1995 Conference on Editorial Problems, the thirty-first in the series, was the first to devote itself to texts composed by women. The participants, who gathered at University College, University of Toronto, on 3 and 4 November, represented several disciplines, but all shared the concern of discovering, or recovering, works by women. Today particularly, when much attention is being paid to revising the established canon of English literature and when women's studies programmes are searching for the 'genuine' voice of women, the focus on writing by women is timely. The papers, given by scholars distinguished in their fields, considered texts written in English in a variety of literary genres covering a period from the fourteenth century to the mid-twentieth.

The publication in 1990 of *The Feminist Companion to Literature in English* was a ground-breaking step towards identifying women writers and in providing biographical information about them.[1] This reference work, and others that have been appearing in recent years, have fostered the next stage of the process, actually bringing to light the marginalized or unheard voices of these women by editing their texts. Until recently, this task has been relatively neglected. The inauguration, however, of series such as Women Writers in English 1350–1850 sponsored by the Brown University Women Writers Project, under the general editorship of Susanne Woods, is helping to recover long-neglected writing by women – as Woods herself has more colourfully made the point, 'there were many "Judith Shakespeares."'[2] We were fortunate that our conference attracted the interest of speakers and delegates who have been prominent among the pioneers engaged in this important work.

The papers were presented in reverse chronological order beginning with feminist critic Joan Coldwell, who in describing her work as editor of Canadian poet and writer Anne Wilkinson (1910–61) initiated discussion of issues surrounding current editing methodology, particularly from a feminist viewpoint. In 'Walking the Tightrope with Anne Wilkinson,' Coldwell discusses past and present editions of Wilkinson's poetry as well as her own editions of the previously unpublished journals and autobiography. Originally motivated by the desire to make available and to reevaluate the work of this once extremely popular, but (until recently) almost forgotten poet, Coldwell offers intriguing insights and raises a number of essential questions faced by women editing women's texts in her frank analysis of her own work as editor. In passing, she notes that these issues have only occasionally been discussed in print.

Questions of the role of gender and of power relations (or control) initiate Coldwell's enquiry into her own work as editor, but, as she sagely notes, 'these questions may be doubled' for they can also be asked of Anne Wilkinson. Besides having published two books of her own poetry, *Counterpoint to Sleep* (1951) and *The Hangman Ties the Holly* (1955), Wilkinson was a founding editor of *The Tamarac Review*, a journal for creative writing, and – even more germane to Coldwell's enquiry – she herself had been involved in the process of editing the journals and correspondence of her own relatives to create a family history, *Lions in the Way* (1956). Thus Coldwell's questions – 'How did her being a woman bear upon [Wilkinson's] poetry and its production? As an editor herself, how did she exercise power over the work of others? And how did the cultural context of her time facilitate or hinder the writing, publishing and reception of her poetry?'[3] – have a special resonance. Moreover, although directed toward her particular subject, many of Coldwell's concerns apply more generally and are taken up by the other speakers.

The title of Naomi Black's paper, ' "Not a novel, they said": Editing Virginia Woolf's *Three Guineas*,' indicates that even a writer as well known as Virginia Woolf (1882–1941) can be momentarily silenced when what she has to say does not conform to a generally acceptable mode. A political theorist with particular interest in feminism and in women's relationship to politics, Black brings her expertise to a discussion of the political situation Woolf is addressing in *Three Guineas*, a work which now, after long neglect, is seen as Woolf's key feminist polemic. In addition, Black speculates about an audience that defied the booksellers' prediction that 'the public won't touch anything controversial about women.'[4] In editing Virginia Woolf, Black faces the added challenge of dealing with an author who was experimenting with literary genre and even with media, in this case photographs of real events with no immediately obvious connection to the 'fictional' text.

One of Black's most pressing problems, however, is what authority to give to any one of the multiplicity of versions which appeared in the evolution of *Three Guineas*. Coldwell too, confronted with two auto-biographical sketches of Anne Wilkinson, cites the work of Donald H. Reiman, whose term 'versioning' describes different stages of a literary work.[5] In the case of Wilkinson's autobiographical writings, Coldwell suggests that she was consciously constructing different selves depending on her intended audience. For Black, matters are less clear, for *Three Guineas* began its published life as a talk and then appeared in six further stages in published form. The question of which version, or versions, should be granted authority arises in the work of each speaker, but this is an important issue for any editor and is not confined to texts by women. As Margaret Anne Doody suggests in her closing remarks, multiple versions may be a problem that modern technology with computers and databases will help solve.

Isobel Grundy, one of the compilers of *The Feminist Companion*, and well known for her work on letter writer, poet, and essayist Lady Mary Wortley Montagu (1689–1762), began the proceedings on Saturday with a tribute to her early mentor, David Fleeman, 'a leader of the new school of editing.' Among other ideas, his notion of the text as 'a process,' rather than 'a single entity' and of the various witnesses as 'merely markers on the continuum of that process' underlie Grundy's recent thoughts on the problems of editing and contribute to the on-going discussion of 'versioning.'[6] In outlining the history of her work on Montagu, which she first undertook as full-time research assistant for Robert Halsband on his edition of the *Complete Letters*, Grundy demonstrates Fleeman's theory of 'text-as-flux' by showing how some of her earlier work has become outdated by the discovery of new material. Now too she challenges notions of 'complete' or 'definitive' editions by questioning their intended audience and the validity of the goals behind such editions. She warns, however, against any feeling of superiority on the part of the modern editor, for at the present time, just as earlier, our goals and practices are shaped by our ideologies and circumstances.

Even with such caveats, Grundy tellingly illustrates further pitfalls presented to the editor of the work of a woman of Montagu's class and time, and especially of a woman whose personal history can be seen as bravely unconventional. In 1712 to escape an imposed marriage, Lady Mary eloped with Edward Wortley Montagu. Four years later she travelled with his embassy to Turkey (1716–18), producing her famous travel-letters. On her return to England, she campaigned to establish smallpox inoculation and wrote brilliant letters of social comment as well as poems on controversial topics such as marriage and divorce. In 1739, she left England apparently for her health, but actually hoping to live with Francesco Algarotti. Although the meeting with Algarotti was a disappointment, Lady Mary remained abroad until her husband's death in 1761. The next year she herself died in London of breast cancer. A certain amount of supression and 'redirection' on the part of an early editor in the pay of Montagu's descendants is thus not entirely surprising, but it has led to subsequent errors and various misconceptions, including wrong birthdate and birthplace. More telling, however, is the reassigning of place of origin to a number of letters, which for years has led Montagu pilgrims to the gracious hospitality of a farm in northern Italy which Montagu never knew. Ironically, as Grundy explains, it is some of the early pirated editions that bring us closest to Montagu's actual writing, and her discussion of Lady Mary's collusion in such 'pirating' illustrates how women were often able to circumvent social pressures.

While Lady Mary may have been able to take some part in orchestrating what Grundy describes as 'her transformation into an author,'[7] Katherine Philips (1632–64), as Germaine Greer indicates in her paper, 'Editorial Conundra in the Texts of Katherine Philips,' seems to have been less successful and more bound by the etiquette of the times in her struggle to achieve her own identity as a writer. Greer, who has worked extensively on women writers in the classical period and in seventeenth-century England,[8] has been engaged in the massive project of recovering and publishing the poetry, letters, translations, and other writings of royalist poet Katherine Philips. One of the few active poets during the decade before the Restoration in 1660, Philips circulated her work in manuscript among a literary coterie (often referred to as a 'Society of Friendship'), whose members were assigned poetic names. Orinda (the name Philips adopted) was celebrated for her expression of Platonic friendship, particularly in poems to Rosania (Mary Aubrey) and Lucasia (Anne Owen), which employ conventions of Metaphysical poetry to evoke ideals of female love, honour, equality and literacy. In response, Jeremy Taylor, for example, dedicated his *Discourse on Friendship* (1657) to Philips. In other poems, Orinda's gift for phrasing and cadence, seen especially in her use of the couplet, was judged by her contemporaries to be innovative. Her translation of Corneille's play *Pompée*, for example, was termed a literary triumph, and even today it is considered the best verse translation of Corneille in English. Her letters to the courtier, Sir Charles Cotterell, later published as *Letters from Orinda to Poliarchus* (1705), have been described as a stage in the development of the epistolary novel. One can thus understand why to her contemporaries Philips came to be known as 'the Matchless Orinda.'

Despite such accolades, the attempt to circulate manuscripts of royalist verse during the Interregnum (1649–60) seems, as Greer has begun to detect, to have given rise to certain conventions in Orinda's coterie, and thus the task of choosing appropriate copy-texts becomes especially complicated. Greer has discovered, for instance, that some poems printed under Philips's name are not by her, that some she corrected or edited herself, that some were edited with her permission, while others may have been changed by an 'improving' editor without her knowledge, and so on. Even autograph manuscripts are not completely reliable, for sometimes Philips can be shown to have copied out or incorporated verses that, as Greer puts it, caught her eye. Moreover, Philips was working in an era and in a circle in which collaboration was the rule and in which young, 'uneducated' talent willingly submitted to 'correction.' As Greer movingly recounts how Philips was forced to disclaim all literary ambition, particularly in the retraction of an edition of her poems in 1664, we are shown that hers was a time when being a gentlewoman meant that a young woman 'could not afford to be seen to exhibit her talents and feelings to the multitude.'[9]

Somewhat later in the same century (1670), the first printed edition of the writings of Julian of Norwich (1342/43 – after 1416) was dismissed by an Anglican cleric as 'the Fanatick Revelations of distempered brains.'[10] Here, of course, factors such as differences in religious belief come into play, but more serious was the fact that a woman was presuming to write about her spiritual insights, for both in the cleric's day and earlier in Julian's time religion was viewed as a strictly male preserve. In the last paper, 'Julian of Norwich and Self-Textualization,' Felicity Riddy discusses the process by which Julian transformed the sixteen visions or 'showings' she experienced during a serious illness in May 1373 when she was thirty-and-a-half years old into verbal form, so that they might be as profitable to others as they had been to her. The transformation occurred in two stages: first, in what has come to be called the Short Text, a fairly immediate description of what Julian terms bodily or spiritual visions or visions given to her understanding, is recorded; then, after an interval of twenty or more years, sustained prayer and meditation on the visions resulted in the Long Text which expands on the spiritual and theological implications of the visions. At the outset, Riddy, although acknowledging that Julian lived in an anchorhold in Norwich, rejects the generally accepted notion that she wrote as a solitary recluse in isolation and shows how this assumption has affected decisions made by earlier editors. Instead, Riddy suggests that in the light of recent studies we need to rethink the role of the anchoress as author and, adopting a model proposed by Jerome McGann, she convincingly argues that Julian's book, *A Revelation of Love*, can be more easily understood as a product of collaboration among writers, scribes, and 'what might be called "clerical facilitators" of various kinds.'[11]

Furthermore, since *A Revelation of Love* exists in a short and a long text, the concept of 'versioning' or 'process,' discussed in relation to Wilkinson and Montagu, pertains also to Julian, but in a somewhat different context. As Riddy points out, the theology in the short version is embryonic in form, while the longer version reflects Julian's further thinking, talking, and rewriting. This latter version Riddy describes as 'a record of a mind in process, not just an achieved statement,' and she discusses how prolongued introspection produces a fluidity in the identities which are recalled.[12] In exploring the transition from shorter to longer text, Riddy emphasizes the importance of the manuscript tradition, indicating in particular the textual significance of the witnesses of the longer text, even though they belong to the seventeenth century. Through a careful examination of these manuscripts, Riddy brings us closer to Julian and her collaborators and to a better understanding of Julian's compositional methods, which she sees as related to Julian's evolving sense of herself as an author, that is, to what Riddy has called the process of 'self-textualization.'

Margaret Anne Doody undertook the task of responding to the five papers with brilliance and flair. Before embarking on her prepared response, she dazzled the packed lecture hall with perceptive off-the-cuff observations of what had actually been discussed during each session. Doody's written text offers astute insights and points to common themes or attitudes voiced by, and problems confronting, each of the Editing Women.

Herself a distinguished editor of women (Fanny Burney [1752–1840] and Jane Austen [1775–1817]), Doody touches on how the experiences of the conference speakers resonate with her own and observes that 'an editor is a kind of highly specialized biographer ..., really a kind of primary biographer.'[13] Similarly, Doody uses her own editorial experience to confirm the frequently mentioned practice of tidying up and rewriting works by women so that, with Germaine Greer, she too warns that it is unlikely that texts attributed to women 'actually represent what women wrote and the way they wrote it.'[14] On the other hand, Doody reminds us that the same can be said of texts by male writers, especially as we go back in time, and she cites note-worthy cases of classical writers and, nearer our own time, difficulties with the texts of Shakespeare and Alexander Pope. Although women writers do indeed deserve special treatment due to their long neglect, Doody looks forward to a future in which editing will more often be a joint enterprise to which women will bring new viewpoints and new expectations. She also predicts that with the simultaneous availability of various textual versions on the computer database, the reader will actually become a kind of secondary editor in being able to combine in new ways materials offered by the primary editor.

NOTES

1   Virginia Blain, Patricia Clements, and Isobel Grundy, *The Feminist Companion to Literature in English: Women Writers from the Middle Ages to the Present* (New Haven and London: Yale University Press, 1990).

2   *The Poems of Aemilia Lanyer: SALVE DEUS REX JUDEORUM*, ed. Susanne Woods, Women Writers in English 1350–1850 (New York: Oxford University Press, 1993), ix.

3   Coldwell, below p. 4.

4   Quoted from a letter to Ethel Smyth, 26 June 1938; see Black, below p. 27 and n2.

5   Donald H. Reiman, *Romantic Texts and Contexts* (Columbia: University of Missouri Press, 1987), esp. 169–70.

6   Grundy, below p. 55.

7   Grundy, below p. 63.

8   Her most recent book, *Slip-Shod Sibyls: Recognition, Rejection and the Woman Poet* (London: Viking, 1995), discusses this work.

9   Greer, below p. 91.

10   Riddy, below p. 101.

11   Riddy, below p. 105.

12   Riddy, below p. 104.

13   Doody, below p. 129.

14   Doody, below p. 134.

Editing Women

In June and Gentle Oven

In June and gentle oven
Summer kingdoms simmer
As they come
And flower and leaf and love
Release
Their sweetest juice.

No wind at all
On the wide green world
Where fields go stroll-
ing by
And in and out
An adder of a stream
Parts the daisies
On a small Ontario farm.

And where, in curve of meadow,
Lovers, touching, lie,
A church of grass stands up
And walls them, holy, in.

Fabulous the insects
Stud the air
Or walk on running water,
Klee-drawn saints
And bright as angels are.

Honeysuckle here
Is more than bees can bear
And time turns pale
And stops to catch its breath
And lovers slip their flesh
And light as pollen
Play on treble water
Till bodies reappear
And a shower of sun
To dry their languor.

Then two in one the lovers lie
And peel the skin of summer
With their teeth
And suck its marrow from a kiss
So charged with grace
The tongue, all knowing
Holds the sap of June
Aloof from seasons, flowing.

JOAN COLDWELL

1 Walking the Tightrope with Anne Wilkinson

'That damn book ... *How* could I, *why* did I think I could do it? The whole thing a nightmare, purposely entered into.'[1] Not my words (though they could have been) but the poet Anne Wilkinson's, as she struggled to edit fifty-years' worth of letters for her family history *Lions in the Way*.[2] In her response to the reader's report and to the 'extensive editorial suggestions' offered by the Macmillan Company, I seemed to hear my own voice as I in turn edited her previously unpublished journals and autobiography: 'Lots of hard work involved. Good. I swing between being exhilarated and appalled at what is before me' (127). It was as if I often found myself mirrored, much as she did in reading Virginia Woolf's *A Writer's Diary*: 'Felt a painful kinship – as if I am her untalented younger sister – but so much her sister, herself, that I could have written the book – if I could write' (115).

In a sense I *did* write the book. I took Anne Wilkinson's manuscripts, altered them, yoked them together, supplied titles, notes, and an introductory essay that invites the reader to add my vision to hers. Editor became more than facilitator or neutral scribe, became a collaborator in Anne Wilkinson's writing of her life. And to the palimpsest were added, of course, the interventions of *my* publisher's readers and editors. Before the text went public, entering that domain of instability where each reader's response makes of it something new every time, it was already multi-authored, a double-triple-quadruple-voiced discourse.

To take up that question, then: *Why* did I tackle the book? In part the answer was again the same as hers ... people kept asking me to do it: 'I said yes from a sense of duty,' she wrote. 'One should have some public responsibility – or should one?' (42). For me, public responsibility had to do with the feminist enterprise of gynocriticism, bringing back to light and re-evaluating the work of women writers that has been obscured, marginalized, or lost. In this project the first task was to help reissue, in 1990, a collected edition of Anne Wilkinson's poetry which had first been published in 1968,[3] and then to write accessible introductions to her work in a reference text and a student handbook.[4] Gynocriticism also leads to reading beyond the boundaries of established genres, finding in so-called subliterary forms like diaries and women's life-stories a rich source of knowledge and insight. Thus my volume entitled *The Tightrope Walker: Autobiographical Writings of Anne Wilkinson* contains diary entries that she had hand-written in seven exercise books[5] and an autobiography whose typescript had been sent to Macmillan Publishers and returned with editorial suggestions for revisions.[6] Terminal illness prevented her from completing these.

The central question in any feminist enquiry is: how does gender operate in whatever system is under scrutiny? That question almost invariably leads to an analysis of power relations: who has control over whom or what, and to what end? In the context of my editing Anne Wilkinson's work the questions can be rephrased (for this enterprise I appropriate the parodic title of Michelene Wandor's book of drama criticism, *Look Back in Gender*):[7]

1 how did the fact that I am a woman affect my role as editor of another woman's text?
2 did I, as a feminist, use the control over the material that every editor has in any way differently from a non-feminist scholar of a more traditional bent?
3 what forces in the cultural context operated for or against the production, circulation, and reception of the book?

Once again, these questions may be doubled, asked of Anne Wilkinson. How did her being a woman bear upon her poetry and its production? As an editor herself, how did she exercise power over the work of others? And how did the cultural context of her time facilitate or hinder the writing, publishing, and reception of her poetry?

My aim in what follows is to explore feminist editorial process, a subject which up to now has only occasionally been discussed in print. The word 'process' seems apt because, as my own feminism changes shape with experience and in light of new feminist theory and practice, I feel compelled to re-edit what is already edited. I don't believe I would adopt – not yet anyway – what I think of as *radical* feminist editorial practices, such as revising spatial arrangements by bringing footnotes up into the body of the text in order to make editorial intervention visible.[8] But I am at the stage of recognizing that I made editorial decisions five years ago that for political reasons I would not make now. I will refer to some of them in passing.

How then did Anne Wilkinson get lost? In the 1950s she had established a strong reputation as an accomplished poet, her two published volumes praised by such luminaries as Northrop Frye, Desmond Pacey, Earl Birney, and A.J.M. Smith. In a sensitive obituary for the *Toronto Star*, Robert Fulford wrote of her 'clear, hard, graceful verse,' of her 'intelligence, wit, humane tolerance, warm generosity.'[9] In addition to two volumes of poetry, she had published *Lions in the Way* (a history of her ancestors), *Swann and Daphne* (a children's book), and a brief autobiographical essay entitled 'Four Corners of My World.' She was fifty years old when she died of lung cancer in 1961.

It is not entirely stating the obvious to say that if she had lived longer she would now be better known. It was an accident of history that she died just before the nationalist fervour of 1965 led to a cultural revolution where Canadian literature was valued and promoted as it had never been before. In her lifetime, strong women writers with international reputations were only just emerging in Canada. She had no chance to go on poetry-reading tours such as those which the Canada Council and other bodies now sponsor, to be a writer-in-residence at a university, or to have the support of the Writers' Union.

Nor did she live beyond the point at which women were still almost entirely dependent on men for a place in the literary world. Men were the 'gatekeepers,'[10] the ones who edited magazines and anthologies, who read manuscripts for publishing houses and decided the academic canon. As the novelist Ethel Wilson tellingly put it, 'These doors were opened to us, poets or writers of prose, by ... men, and if we would, and could, we passed through the doors into the open air of speech and communication.'[11]

Anne Wilkinson learned her craft with the help of male poets; although she was acquainted with several women poets – P.K. Page, Phyllis Webb, Margaret Avison – she seems never to have sought their professional advice. Journals and letters record her gratitude to the men who advised her: F.R. Scott, Earle Birney, A.J.M. Smith, Louis Dudek. Alan Crawley, the west coast editor of *Contemporary Verse*, was a particularly helpful mentor; Dorothy Livesay once spoke on the radio of his influence on Anne Wilkinson and others: 'there must be at least seven Canadian women poets who went to him for help, sent their material to him and got a great deal of encouragement ... it's just amazing how particularly the *young* women seemed to get a stimulus from him.'[12]

Anne Wilkinson: 'Coming Out' portrait 1928 (photo given to Joan Coldwell by Alan Gibbons).

Grateful though Anne Wilkinson was for such benevolent influences on her poetry, there was an aspect of this male patronage that worked against her literary career. Mary Ellmann long ago pointed out that men seem unable to distinguish between a woman's body and her writing, so that their assessment of her poetry often amounts to 'an intellectual measuring of busts and hips.'[13] Anne Wilkinson was physically beautiful and very attractive to men. As a result, sex and text sometimes seemed inextricably linked. 'Un-maiden-with bright- and beautiful-poet-head!' is the salutation on a letter from one mentor.[14] Another writes of 'the beautiful smile that comes into your eyes, and it is of them I am reminded on reading your verse.'[15] What may happen with such conflation is that once the body is gone, the poetry may be forgotten also.

When men were inevitably the medium for survival in the literary marketplace, the beautiful female body could be considered capital likely to attract interest. Anne Wilkinson's diaries record the exhilara- tion of love affairs with at least three of the men who published or promoted her work, and the disillusionment and emptiness when those sources of inspiration dried up: 'Low and lonely ... Had time for someone I loved, who I felt was a part of the strange creative process. I miss him more than I can say; my imagination is quite desolate. But I do not want to be one of his sad crew of women, threatening suicide, having nervous breakdowns, all of them artists who should be working and can't. I would rather live and work than moan away my days' (133).

One of these sentences ('But I do not want to be one of his sad crew of women ...') was deleted in the manuscript. Why did I change the author's mind for her by reinstating it? I believe I was reacting at the time to the fact that a full-scale biography of the man in question had recently appeared with no reference to any one of his 'crew of women.' It seemed to me to distort the portrait of the man to ignore completely an activity that obviously took up a good deal of his time and energy, and to overlook contributions those women possibly made to *his* poetic development, to erase them from literary history. Perhaps I was motivated too by a kind of puritanical resistance to the way a false image of the man's monogamous marriage bolsters sexual hypocrisy, still such a feature of Canadian life. A prissy, holier-than-thou stand, maybe, but I stick to it. I would, however, now show the sentence as a deletion: I believe in that form it would make even more of a forceful statement about silencing, self-censorship, and the social context.

Anne Wilkinson's lovers were also the editors who selected poems for anthologies. It is small wonder, then, that the most frequently anthologized piece was her extremely sensuous love poem 'In June and gentle oven.' I quote a part of it:

> Honeysuckle here
> Is more than bees can bear
> And time turns pale
> And stops to catch its breath
> And lovers slip their flesh
> And light as pollen
> Play on treble water
> Till bodies reappear
> And a shower of sun
> To dry their langour.
>
> Then two in one the lovers lie
> And peel the skin of summer
> With their teeth
> And suck its marrow from a kiss
> So charged with grace
> The tongue, all knowing
> Holds the sap of June
> Aloof from seasons, flowing.[16]

It is a lovely poem but it gives a one-sided, and not particularly representative, view of her style. It marks her as a starry-eyed romantic, absorbed in supposedly typical women's concerns.

In considering the rise or decline of a writer's reputation, it is fruitful to take into account the power of the anthology not only to canonize but also to determine ways of reading. For example, another of Anne Wilkinson's most frequently anthologized poems is the one that begins 'I am so tired I do not think/Sleep in death can rest me.'[17] Those who lost a friend and lover when Anne Wilkinson died naturally found this poem particularly moving. They read it in light of her death, as if it were one of her last poems; it was, in fact, one of her earliest. Fine poem though this too is, it helps to enforce a stereotype of the woman poet as delicate invalid, an Elizabeth Barrett who rises from her couch only for a Prince Charming to whom she can pen 'How do I love thee? Let me count the ways.' Barrett Browning's major strengths as a writer, hailed in her own time but ignored until feminist critics brought *Aurora Leigh* back to light, were obscured by the anthologizing of pieces that comfortably fit a stereotype of weak, feeble, and adoring woman.

Even the most perceptive of Anne Wilkinson's critics seem unable to separate her from domesticity. Kildare Dobbs, as an editor for Macmillan, wrote a long commentary on the manuscript of her second book, probably the most sensitive and thoughtful analysis of her work I have seen. He uses terms such as 'carefully managed syntactical surprises,' 'piercing precision,' 'subtlety,' 'metre that everywhere enforces the sense,' 'depths below depths of meaning,' then, lo and behold, concludes that her poetry reads as if 'she seems to be no more than humming as she does the dishes.'[18]

Earle Birney wrote a review for CBC radio, of which the draft version as well as the broadcast one exists. He praised her work above Irving Layton's. For this misdemeanour he reported that 'Layton has sent his "undying hatred" and threatens to consult a lawyer.'[19] In the draft version, Birney wrote of Anne Wilkinson's poetic 'music, either simple as the nursery rhymes she sometimes draws on, or intellectually patterned as a fugue.' What he actually said in the broadcast, in a supposedly shortened version, was 'When she comes home from a walk, she casually shakes a shower of images off in the hall, and proceeds to play music, from lilting nursery rhymes to the most patterned of fugues.'[20] Note that what has been sacrificed to economy is the word 'intellectually'; what has been added at some length is the image of a lady of leisure, on whom poetry mercifully drops like the gentle rain from heaven.

It is perhaps not surprising that Birney could think of Anne Wilkinson only in a domestic setting, woman's supposedly proper place. He it was who kept a card index of contributors to his magazine *Canadian Poetry*, with thumb-nail sketches to remind himself of who was who. Anne Wilkinson appears as 'Tor[onto] housewife, without a univ[ersity] education,' a put-down for any poet and coming from Birney a triple condemnation. Only those who have lived in western Canada can fully appreciate the scorn conveyed by the word 'Toronto.' Certainly in the 1950s it was still a parochial and puritanical place. 'How dull are the facts of everyday in Toronto' (60), Anne Wilkinson herself wrote and she devised 'a test of true love for a Torontonian: If you can walk down Yonge St. with your beloved and still think man's world is a thing of beauty, it's love. I can't' (11). Montreal was the lively centre of poetic activity and it was when she was introduced to the circle of poets there that Anne Wilkinson felt she had come into a writers' world.

Birney's phrase 'without a university education' smacks of élitism and implies that Anne Wilkinson was a female version of the Ploughman Poet. Certainly she missed some of the useful side-effects of academic life, such as having a circle of like-minded friends to share the interests of a beginning writer. But it is misleading to imply that she was uneducated; she was indeed largely *self*-educated but she read extremely widely, intelligently, and critically, as the diaries attest. One of the strengths, and the complexities, of her poetry may be said to stem from her idiosyncratic choice of reading. There is a freshness and originality about her images that derives perhaps from such idiosyncrasy and that might have been stifled had she been fed a conventional curriculum, heavy with canonical texts.

The most patronizing noun in Birney's sketch is also the least accurate. If 'housewife' conjures the image of dishpan hands wielding a duster, nothing could be further from the truth. I doubt if Anne Wilkinson ever washed a dish or held a duster in her life. Just once her writing was interrupted by the fact that her cook was ill and she was obliged to learn how to open a can: 'O dear, the food and produce is so inclined to concrete. My shame on the matter is not as great as it once was. Why should a poet be a cook? I do not demand that my cook be also a poet' (91).

Anne Wilkinson came from a wealthy family where there were always people to take care of the mechanics of living: cooks, gardeners, chauffeurs, nannies, seamstresses, governesses, and maids. If the household of her married life was scaled down from the grand style of the house in which she had grown up, she nevertheless always had resident help that gave her a freedom to write enjoyed by very few 'housewives.'

I am glad to have moved this far into my paper before mentioning the fact that Anne Wilkinson was a descendant of the socially prominent Osler family. She was a grand-daughter of Sir Edmund Osler, MP, founder of the brokerage firm of Osler and Hammond, president of the Dominion Bank, director of the Canadian Pacific Railway, generous donor to the Royal Ontario Museum and, in the gift of Craigleigh Gardens Park, to the city of Toronto. It was in the grand Edwardian world of his mansion, Craigleigh, that she spent several of her childhood years. In his company, too, she visited an even more distinguished relative, great-uncle Sir William Osler, Regius Professor of Medicine at Oxford, who in addition to his well-deserved fame as a physician, was widely reputed to have advocated euthanasia for everyone over sixty!

It is too easy to draw attention to Anne Wilkinson as an Osler rather than as a poet. One anthology, for example, offers a brief introduction to each writer: Roy Daniells is introduced as 'a formalist, a writer of quiet measured lines'; 'Alden Nowlan writes of small-town life with the same harshness and ironic stress that other poets apply to the big city'; and so on. Anne Wilkinson is introduced only as 'a descendant of the Osler family.'[21] The subtext here is that the family connection is of more interest than the poetry, perhaps even that the poetry is valued only because of the family.

One of the most revised passages in the autobiography tackles this very point. It takes several rewritings for Wilkinson to capture the nuances of people's response to the family connections and her own ambivalence about them. In describing her arrival at the Ojai School in California she writes that everyone is captivated by her mother: 'They treat her royally, a tribute to her beauty and intelligence, but they also know her as a niece of Sir William Osler, still a popular memory here in the United States and this plays a part, a fact of which we are not unaware' (the word 'memory' replaces 'hero,' and the reference to Sir William is further diluted by omitting a phrase about his recently published biography). How could we be unaware, she asks, 'having lived our lives as children of grandfathers, great-nieces and great-nephew of imposing great-uncles? Thanks to Canadian Pacific connections we never travel in Canada or the U.S. without word being sent ahead to insure that we are specially cared for. No queuing for meals, and only the most courtly attention from custom and immigration officials. Everything oiled.' Then follows a much-amended analysis of the 'two minds' she found herself in. 'It embarrassed me; I believed I hated it. I wanted to hate it, yet I did not, for I had come to depend on special attention, something easy enough to scorn in theory, but in practice an almost universal pleasure ... At the Ojai School I made a first attempt to unfamily my family self' (181).

It is well nigh impossible to 'unfamily' Anne Wilkinson, to separate her work from her family, both her Osler ancestors and her immediate circle of mother, husband, and three children. Her first published volume, *Counterpoint to Sleep*, begins with 'Summer Acres,' a poem of homage to the ancestors who spent their summers at Roches Point, the family estate on Lake Simcoe:

> These acres breathe my family,
> Holiday with seventy summers' history.
> My blood lives here,

> Sunned and veined three generations red
> Before my bones were formed.[22]

Family is the subject of numerous poems, from those describing children's summer swimming to those obliquely charting the disintegration of her marriage or mourning the death of her mother. In addition, she edited family papers to create *Lions in the Way* and wrote an autobiography which places herself always in the family context and particularly in relation to her mother.

Although she was deeply attached to her family, she sometimes felt overwhelmed and oppressed by it, especially when writing the history: 'To write a book about one's family is a more hazardous undertaking, psychologically, than I had realized ... I need to escape, in work, *from* my family. Instead, my work *is* the family. I feel smothered, all but annihilated, by *family, family, family*' (136).

Here is another sentiment I sometimes shared. It was not an easy task to identify the members of a huge and close-knit extended family who bore the same names over the generations, two Wilmot Matthews, for example, three George Gibbons, and two different Dr Harrisons mentioned within one three-line passage. Surviving members of Anne Wilkinson's immediate family had initiated the project of publishing the journals and were extremely generous with their help. For them too, though, it was sometimes a pyschologically 'hazardous undertaking,' reviving painful memories or presenting versions of the past that did not chime with their own recollections. As editor I felt I occasionally became the whipping girl for hurts of long ago.

One justification I offered to myself for publishing so private a document was that the journals give a great deal of insight into the tensions of a woman writer who is also a mother, insight that might help others in the same situation: 'Being a mother and being a poet, both need a lot of getting away from,' Anne Wilkinson wrote (63). To focus on this, however, might enforce just such an image of domesticity as I was castigating in male critics. Women poets, it might suggest, do not produce significant work and lack dedication to art because someone is always demanding attention, some stranger from Porlock always knocking at the door. It is too easy to overlook the strengths women have drawn from such situations, in perfecting the 'snapshot' poem, as Adrienne Rich did, or in making a short story out of those very interruptions and demands, as Alice Munro did in 'The Office.'[23] And Anne Wilkinson astutely observed that maternal obligations sometimes offer a fine excuse for procrastination: 'have been so preoccupied with domestic affairs that I had almost forgotten that I used to try and write verse. The next month looks just as full, with dentist's appointments for three children, summer shopping, rushing ... to instruct painters and carpenters ... I expect the truth of the matter is that I don't want to write at the moment – if I did I'd find time even if it meant letting the children's teeth rot!'[24]

Most editors of diaries and personal letters experience a *crise de conscience* over publication of works not meant for the public eye. Feminists object also to what is termed 'appropriation of voice,' which in this case takes the form of making decisions for the author whether she might have liked them or not. At times I convinced myself that Anne Wilkinson *did* want the diaries read. There is anecdotal evidence that she burned some of her autobiographical writing, but she didn't, after all, destroy the diaries. And there is often evidence of careful stylistic revision and self-conscious shaping. Much as I would like to think this argues awareness of audience, I believe these are the marks of a writer practising her craft.

What then is the justification, and specifically the feminist justification, for publishing the journals? In my introduction I wrote: 'The first, and perhaps to many the only convincing, reply is the service of literature' (xv). I squirm now at that phrase. There was the voice of one trained in the new critical school, proclaiming the gospel of art for art's sake. I no longer believe (probably I didn't then either) in an abstract 'literature' that demands service of its disciples. Quite the opposite: literature serves its makers, both authors of the texts and their readers. This might bring me to the same point I so clumsily made in the edition, that reading the diaries illumines the poetry, sometimes making difficult images clearer, sometimes showing the relationship of poems to specific moments of her life. (This, however, might in turn enforce a hierarchical ordering of genres that I would wish to resist: the humble diary the handmaiden of poetry, rather than a work of value in itself, a genre whose difference requires appraisal by quite other standards than the comparative.)

Having decided to let the unspoken speak, I could see no reason to leave anything out. There is evidence over and over again in the journals that Anne Wilkinson lived in a world of polite silences and glossings-over that sometimes caused her a great deal of grief. To the general context of the silencing of women was added the family's extraordinary belief in the virtues of reticence. Just once the well-mannered facade of concealment cracked and her sense of fun revelled in the result. It was at a family dinner party at the sedate York Club:

The evening quickly assumed an air of wildest fantasy. Cocktails –
champagne – liqueurs reduced to nil the inhibitions of the elders. The
sisters-in-law, Aunt Amo and Aunt Maggie, old women who had held
their tongues (ahem!) for fifty years, suddenly let forth with the stuff
that dreams are made of. Resentments politely concealed for decades
spouted like burst hydrants. Neither listened to anything ... They were
mad with the taste on their tongues of things too long left unsaid. But
such brave spirited fighting cocks – it is impossible to call them hens
– made the whole affair a tragi-comedy. They kept, for the most part,
their wit and thrust. I was reduced to helpless, hilarious laughter.
What an airing of the bedclothes. What a picture of their various,
though linked pasts ... O it was a glorious brawl and I doubt that
harm will come of it, that anyone will bear resentment. They behaved
outrageously but something in our nature feels in the outrage a
catharsis. And it was done with sets and props, it was on the stage.
We called our cabs and dispersed to our immediate homes (123–4).

I hope it is not an outrage to have printed the diaries; at the very least,
I hope with their author that no harm will come of it. I cling to the
more positive belief, though, that it enlarges our understanding of one
another and ourselves to read the intimate details of personal lives
different in kind and degree from our own.

It was at the family's request that I edited the journals. It was
entirely my own decision to add to them the unpublished autobiography found in the Thomas Fisher Rare Book Library at the University
of Toronto. The book was planned at a time when there was considerable critical and theoretical interest in the different forms that life-
writing can take, and especially in the ways in which women's auto-
biographies might differ from men's. To put diaries and autobiography
together is to show alternative ways of constructing a self, in different
but related forms. As I put it in the introduction: 'Whereas the journals
offer random, highly personal and spontaneous reflections on self,
poetry, family, and society, the autobiography consciously and artistically contrives to create a distanced self, the result of that private
scrutiny' (xiv).

Placing the journals first in the book, followed by autobiography,
was a deliberate rejection of chronological story-telling. The diaries
were written between 1947 and 1956, the years of Anne Wilkinson's
productivity as a poet, coinciding with the period she called 'nightmare and strain' as her marriage slowly fell apart. The autobiography
creates a portrait of the artist as a young woman, from birth to
marriage. Interestingly, though, the author of the autobiography does

not organize her life in chronological sequence either. The story of her birth in 1920 is not told until the beginning of chapter three, by which time we have heard about her schooldays in California and the death of her mother in 1956, with an analysis also of her own nature worship as an adult. It is as if linear time is of far less importance in recording a woman's life than an awareness of patterns and their intricate inter-relationships. I resisted some pressure from the publishers to impose a semblance of linear time on the life-story by pointing out that readers could start at the middle of the book if they chose. For my part, I wanted to read the texts in order of composition, to see how private diaries fed into a life constructed for public view.

For the autobiography, Anne Wilkinson created a heavily edited version of her self as 'villain.' She depicted a naughty schoolgirl almost expelled from even the most progressive of schools, a wild adventurer who attempted escapades far beyond her ability to carry through, a prankster who could always be counted on to flout authority. What-ever grain of truth there might be in this portrait, it smacks of wish-fulfilment, a picaresque rebellion against the strict good manners and rigid conventions of the Oslers.

This fictive persona lends weight to Sidonie Smith's theorizing of women's autobiography. Smith argues that a woman, conditioned to self-effacement, accommodates herself to this fundamentally andro-centric, self-promotional genre by assuming 'the adventurous posture of man,' casting her story in the familiar tropes of male selfhood, as here villain, prankster, and picaro, in order to stake a claim in the male-dominated world of words.[25] Pulling against this 'patrilineal contract' is the woman autobiographer's identification with her mother and thence with the muted ideologies of the feminine.

Every chapter of *The Tightrope Walker* begins with a reference, direct or oblique, to Anne Wilkinson's mother. The first is especially telling, for it begins with a womb-like, pre-Oedipal episode focusing on her mother's individual 'flowery smell' and the rhythms of her breath, conflated with the exhalations of the waves (165). The original passage was much longer: the cuts were made because her publisher's reader thought it too early in the text for an essay on smells. Interestingly, though, Anne Wilkinson seems to have developed from her own mem-ory a theory that has since been legitimized by psychologists and others who study the mother-infant link and conclude that smell is one of the chief bonding agents in infancy.

In a sense, the entire narrative is a search for the lost Eden of female connectedness, a world evoked in fluid images of lake water and ocean. Her inability to weep at her mother's funeral is as much a symbolic as realistic drought, an awareness that her source of inspiration had dried up as well as her tears: 'a drought so dry that had I been turned upside down and shaken no tears would have fallen from my eyes' (233).

Water images haunt her poetry too, and in one journal passage she, as it were, psychoanalyzes her intense absorption: '["Lake Song"] is the first love poem I have written and the lover is the sound of lake water! Is the cradle the thing I seek? A cradle to sleep in, not a cradle to rock' (18).

The Lacanian–Kristevan concept of the pre-Oedipal phase of child development and the later 'mirror stage' also helps to account for Anne Wilkinson's intense attachment to her mother and her ambivalence towards her role as poet in a man's world. Lacan proposed that gender differentiation occurs when a child becomes aware of its own identity, its self, from seeing its mirrored reflection. A boy sees his difference from the mother and moves into the separate world of the Fathers, the realm of the Symbolic where phallus is the signifier of male hegemony, of the patriarchal Word. Being *like* her mother, a girl does not separate from her, is always in a world of relationship, and, lacking the phallic Signifier, is forever excluded from the realm of the Symbolic. In reaction to this theory, feminist pyschoanalysts, philosophers, and critics conceive of an alternative discourse of marginality, an *écriture féminine*, marked by the fragmentation, word-play, and fluidity so apparent in Anne Wilkinson's work.

Although the autobiography was not published in her lifetime, her very severely edited version of it appeared as 'Four Corners of My World' in *The Tamarack Review* soon after she died.[26] She had been a founding editor and financial patron of that literary magazine. She acted as poetry editor too, though it was not, as Robert Fulford noted, a comfortable role for her: 'her feelings of sympathy toward other poets made it agony for her to return unusable manuscripts.'[27] 'Four Corners of My World' was reprinted as an epilogue to her *Collected Poems*, edited by A.J.M. Smith in 1968.[28]

The existence of this memoir allows for what Donald Reiman called 'versioning,' the provision of 'complete texts of two or more different stages of a literary work, each of which can be read as an integral whole.'[29] It is apparent that the shortened version subscribes to the 'patrilineal contract' (indeed, at an early stage she had contemplated calling her autobiography *The Grandfathers*). The published title of the memoir points to what now directed her editorial decisions in shortening the work. 'Four Corners of My World' shifts the focus entirely to places and the family connections with them. Instead of the words 'I lay beside my mother' which open the full-length story, we have the de-personalized 'Three houses dominated our London (Ontario) world.'[30] 'London,' 'Roches Point,' 'Toronto,' and 'California' are the section headings; the last word is 'Craigleigh.' Gone is the vigorous depiction of a lively protagonist in the family drama. The voice is that of a well-informed docent leading a tour of historic houses.

Since the full autobiography survives in a near-complete typescript to which some changes had already been made in response to a reader's suggestions, there were not many editorial problems – no handwriting to be deciphered, few unusual references to be footnoted, no characters to be identified. The one difficulty lay with what is obviously an unrevised final chapter from which some pages are missing; frustrating since these are needed to finish a dramatic story of a potential shipwreck. The final sentences, though, are already polished. They are clearly designed to echo a convention of Victorian novels, where a woman is offered a choice between two suitors. The choice made, the rest is silence.

Even though the text of the autobiography was relatively unprob-lematic, it was here that I became most obviously the intrusive editor. The chapter headings are phrases I chose from within each section, a critical and controlling act, since I highlighted what I saw to be of key significance in the text. I have already read one paper where, despite my disclaimers, a point is made about Anne Wilkinson's subtlety in her choice of chapter headings.[31] I think they are, if not subtle, certainly catchy, appropriate, and indeed her own words.

It was her own words, too, that I chose for the title of the whole book. *The Tightrope Walker* is a phrase she used of herself in her journals: 'I've always been a tightrope walker (a foolish occupation for one terrified of heights)' (66). That she liked the image is clear from her use of it in poetry:

> High as fear
> The tightrope,
> Thin as silk the string
> My feet are walking walking[32]

These quotations provided some justification for my choice. In diary, autobiography, and poems Anne Wilkinson often cast herself in the role of entertainer, sometimes as clown. Furthermore, she habitually saw herself as balancing between two poles, of emotions (despair and joy), of inherited family characteristics (romantic and classical), and of the duties of motherhood against the dictates of her art. But I am aware that in selecting this title, and in now offering an explanation of it, I direct readers to a preconception about the text and the life it presents. Furthermore, I bolstered my reading by starting the introduction with another journal quotation in the same vein: 'I am constantly in love with life and always on the brink of despair' (128). I then identified some of what I refer to as dichotomies and dualities. By this means I created the Anne Wilkinson I find in the text. That she is by no means everyone's Anne Wilkinson was brought home to me recently when one acquaintance of the poet objected to the book 'because this was not the Anne she knew.'[33] Here was an insistence on a past which the objector could not recognize as itself a fictional construct, what Audre Lorde has called bio-*mytho*graphy.[34]

Of course, as critics and teachers we are in the business of suggesting ways of reading and I don't mean to imply that there is anything unhelpful about seeing the text through the lens of this particular tightrope image. The danger lies for myself in closing my mind to other readings, and for others in accepting mine as authoritative, the 'right' way to approach the text. In other words, the editor/critic's subject position plays a significant part in the way the material is presented. When, for example, A.J.M. Smith published his *Collected Poems of Anne Wilkinson*, he used for his introduction an essay written soon after her early death, in the shadow of his grief for the woman who had been his close friend and lover. His reading emphasized the poetry's sensuousness, so evocative of the woman he had known, and his horror at what seemed to him to be prophesies of suffering and death. For some considerable time after this, poems were chosen for anthologies and occasional critical comment in the light of this reading.

Would the title Anne Wilkinson herself used have been preferable? I do think *The Tightrope Walker* has more flair than her own *A Curate's Egg*, which suffers from a rather dreary ecclesiastical tone and completely loses its impact when the source of the joke is unknown. It was a long time before I could find anyone to interpret the phrase for me. Since then, it seems I hear it quite often, especially in England: 'Good in parts, like the curate's egg.' It comes from a *Punch* cartoon: a curate, asked by his Bishop if the breakfast egg is to his liking and embarrassed to say that it is bad, replies that 'Parts of it are excellent.' I like the ironic ambiguity implicit in this as title: is it the text that is good in parts, or Anne Wilkinson's life? But although I acknowledge having usurped her author-ity here, I make bold to assume that she too would have approved both the pertinent carnivalesque and the potentially greater marketability of the new title.

To the two forms of journal and autobiography, *The Tightrope Walker* adds yet another in the shape of letters exchanged between the poet and her dying mother. These were included at the request of Anne Wilkinson's younger son, her literary executor, and originally against my own wishes, as I found them painful and intimate in the extreme. They do, however, speak volumes about this particular mother–daughter relationship, so central to the writing of her life, and make a link between the journal, where she fell silent for fourteen months after her mother died, and the autobiography which she wrote in tribute to her.

Although Anne Wilkinson craved men's admiration and love, and needed their help to survive in the literary world, she acknowledged that her greatest strengths came from women: her favourite writers Jane Austen and Virginia Woolf, her close friend and confidante Muriel Douglas, 'the dearest companion imaginable,' and, above all, her mother and aunts, of whom she wrote that it was 'a heaven sent blessing to have been born in the radius of their light' (38). Occasionally she showed some resentment about society's different expectations of men and women: 'the family *should* be enough to absorb her. A hobby is permitted but not a passion. Man, on the other hand, takes his family as a side line and is free from censure or guilt to pursue his life's work' (65). Most often, however, she reveals her insecurity about a presumptuous aspiration to succeed in a patriarchal world: 'I am a woman waiting in a station ... avoid the ticket-master who would ask, where to?' 'I write an inward jargon of a woman barricaded with cardboard' (34).

Whatever insecurities she betrayed in the journals, she held her own when the ticket-masters did suggest directions. She agonized over what response *Lions in the Way* might receive from the Macmillan Company, dreading the 'painful thorns of criticism' and wondering, 'if they say nay how will I make myself go on?' (136). The company said 'yea' but sent her the report of an Unidentified Reader. In her response she referred to him as the U.R.:

> I am now trying to revise the book from the point of view of the U.R.
> (in most respects) and I must know whether all his (her) ideas
> coincide with those of the Macmillan Co. ... Some statements of the
> U.R. seem to me in direct contradiction to remarks made by you and
> Mr. Gray and I would like to get everything as cut and dried as

possible. Mr. Gray gave me the impression that he wanted the bits of
narrative written with a light touch ... the U.R. demands something
else again – well-rounded pictures of the people involved. To me,
except in the hands of a great writer, wellrounded pictures often seem
as dull as billiard balls; interesting protuberances and convexities all
sacrificed to wellroundedness. A small writer is more apt to find
success by throwing a light on an angle of a situation or a person.
Nonetheless I will do what I can along the line he suggests if it is also
Macmillan's line.

Another statement 'there are too many letters ...' leaves me a little
bewildered because I thought the book was nothing *but* letters, the
edited letters of a family. This point must be cleared up. What am I
supposed to be doing? Editing letters, writing a biography, or a historical novel, based on fact? ... I cannot write a book that belongs to
another.[35]

Once again I hear strains of my own voice, when in turn I read the
responses of the URs to *The Tightrope Walker*. No doubt you are all
familiar with the bewilderment of finding comments that are 'in direct
contradiction' with one another. Thus Reader A of my manuscript
found it to be 'exciting,' 'absorbing,' 'extraordinary,' 'beautifully
written,' and 'an important contribution to our literary history'; 'I
highly recommend that this book be published.' Reader B thought it
'not valuable enough to publish,' 'gossipy,' 'of uneven quality,' and
'not particularly significant.' Fortunately, Reader C thought it on the
contrary 'a very significant contribution.' Naturally I do not know the
gender of these readers, but certainly Reader B betrays a patriarchal
attitude in dismissing women's diaries instead of valuing them, as they
should be valued, precisely because they are gossipy. There is, I feel,
a telling detail in Reader B's comment that it is only poetry and not
life-writings that merit a 'place in the canon.'

The many press reviews of *The Tightrope Walker* were, I'm glad to
say, uniformly positive and appreciative. Has Anne Wilkinson, then,
been widely acclaimed as the fine writer she is? Has the lost been
found? I wish I could answer with a resounding affirmative, but in
truth I cannot. One reason, I believe, is the fact that the book did not
reach a large student or general feminist readership. Despite my steady
request to the Press, and the recommendations of its readers, for a
paperback publication, the book appeared only in hardcover. The
$39.95 price, plus tax, virtually guaranteed that it was out of reach of
those who would most have profited from it. I suspect too that Anne

Wilkinson's son, her literary executor, saw no reason to push for a paperback. For him, the book was likely to appeal mostly to family members, especially those who found their names in the index. To them, the volume would be both affordable and worth its price.

Money and social class are perhaps at issue in another area too. Just as Anne Wilkinson missed the opportunities that came to Canadian writers in the seventies, her work is now brought out at a time when feminist eyes are turned to different margins and minorities. The writings of women of colour, third world women, lesbians, and working class women jusitifiably occupy critical attention so that, as Carolyn Heilbrun has said, it is 'not without trepidation' in these times that one argues a case for engagement with the writings of 'middle and upper class, married white women.' Heilbrun, nevertheless, does argue a case, pointing out that 'voicelessness and oppression are linked among the privileged as well as among those oppressed by race and class' and that 'male violence cuts across all races and classes'. She refers to the American poet Maxine Kumin, whose circumstances were similar to Anne Wilkinson's: a late start to writing poetry and later still for writing autobiographical prose. Kumin's words might have been Anne Wilkinson's own: 'I was programmed into one kind of life, which was to say, get ... married, and have a family ... And I came to poetry as a way of saving myself because I was so wretchedly discontented, and I felt so guilty about being discontented.'[36] Heilbrun's conclusion, certainly applicable to Anne Wilkinson's case, is that analysis of such guilt and discontent 'may tell as much about deprived female destiny as do accounts of suffering from the sterner and more obvious forms of oppression.'[37]

Just as in her lifetime Anne Wilkinson depended on men for public acceptance of her work, so now it is, once again, via a male author that most attention has come. In 1984, before *The Tightrope Walker* appeared in print, Michael Ondaatje heard a radio broadcast about Anne Wilkinson in which some brief passages from her journals were read. With cavalier high-handedness Ondaatje took verbatim quotations to put into the mouth of a fictional Anne in his 1987 novel *In the Skin of a Lion*.[38] In an interesting essay on the intertextuality of this novel, Katherine Acheson claims that 'the works of Anne Wilkinson draw out meanings relevant to the themes of the novel, and enrich and complicate the scenes in which the references are made.' These meanings focus, as Acheson's subtitle has it, on 'writing and reading class,' on 'the relationship between the wealthy and the working classes with which the novel is fundamentally concerned.'[39]

Like Anne Wilkinson, Ondaatje comes from a well-off, imperialist family. What kind of bridge can be thrown between one such as himself and the workers who are his subject? As the meta-author within the text, the fictional Anne hints at the possibility of that bridge. She appears in just one episode of the novel, where the thief Caravaggio breaks into her Lake Simcoe boathouse and finds that, for a member of the privileged class, she is surprisingly generous and sympathetic. Ironically, given the obscuring of Anne Wilkinson's reputation, the fictional Anne is read by Acheson as representing 'the narrative hegemony of the ruling class,' with a questionable assertion that 'only the stories of the rich are written down and become history.' Although this essay offers useful insights into the 'thematic and metaphoric alliances between Ondaatje's work and Wilkinson's poetry,' it is curiously unaware of Anne Wilkinson as the diarist whose voice is appropriated. In the prefatory matter, Ondaatje acknowledged that he had taken two sentences verbatim from the journals, but when Acheson quotes those sentences she writes: 'This describes, with Ondaatje's customary brevity and accuracy, one of Wilkinson's early poems.'[40]

Whose brevity and accuracy? We have come full circle, for I started this paper with an assertion that Anne Wilkinson's words became my words, and now they are Ondaatje's, and then Acheson's, and so on *ad infinitum*. With a further kind of intertextuality, I see in the bridge-building of Ondaatje's novel a parallel to my/our metaphor of the tightrope. The bridge over the Don Valley linked the prosperous enclaves of Anglo-Saxon Toronto, epitomized by Anne Wilkinson's Rosedale, with the working-class immigrant neighbourhoods along the Danforth. To edit the personal writings of a woman whose social position and way of life were worlds apart from my own was for me also a bridging experience. I never met Anne Wilkinson and if I had I doubt we would have found a common place to stand. That place is clearly there, in, among many things, what she has to say about being a woman in a man's world, about physical health and spiritual well-being, about the need for laughter, about the love of nature and of home, and above all about mother and daughter.

There is a delightful etching by Henry Moore that serves as an emblem of my experience as Anne Wilkinson's editor. Called 'High Wire Walkers,' it shows two women approaching one another on a tightrope. There is gaiety in the unfurled umbrellas that seem to be about to make them airborne (Mary Poppins comes to mind) but their feet are firm on the wire. One woman holds out her hand to the other. What I cherish most about the image, though, is that the women are naked: bodies are shown in careful detail, but the faces are featureless. In walking the tightrope with Anne Wilkinson, I came close to knowing her without the public face, without the superficial disguises and costumes of the self shown to the world, and I was forced to shed my own prejudices to find myself mirrored in her. But like the figures on Keats's urn, Moore's two women will be forever just about to meet. I don't delude myself that the knowledge could ever be anywhere near complete, or other than a construct I have made myself.

To read of other women's lives, especially in their own voices, is to be given a fuller understanding of ourselves. It is to participate in a community of women writers and readers that generates a different kind of confidence than is permitted to women's voices in patriarchal culture. Thus, with and through Anne Wilkinson, I feel

[That] I am two times born
And when a new moon cuts the night
Or full moons froth with my
And witches' milk

I walk the tightrope
Free and easy as an angel
Toes as certain of their line of silk
As the sturdy ones
Whose feet are curled on earth.[41]

NOTES

1 Anne Wilkinson, *The Tightrope Walker: Autobiographical Writings of Anne Wilkinson*, ed. Joan Coldwell (Toronto: University of Toronto Press, 1992), 137, 136. All subsequent references to journals and autobiography are to this volume.

2 Anne Wilkinson, *Lions in the Way* (Toronto: Macmillan, 1956).

3 Anne Wilkinson, *The Poetry of Anne Wilkinson*, ed. Joan Coldwell (Toronto: Exile Editions, 1990).

4 Joan Coldwell, 'Anne Wilkinson,' in *The Oxford Companion to Canadian Literature*, ed. William Toye (Toronto: Oxford University Press, 1983), 831–2; Joan Coldwell, 'Anne Wilkinson,' in *Profiles in Canadian Literature 7*, ed. Jeffrey Heath (Toronto: Dundurn, 1991), 103–10.

5 Now in the possession of her son Alan Wilkinson, her literary executor.

6 Now housed in the Thomas Fisher Rare Book Library of the University of Toronto.

7 Michelene Wandor, *Look Back in Gender: Sexuality and the Family in Post-War British Drama* (London: Methuen, 1987).

8 See Patricia S. White, 'Black and White and Read All Over: A Meditation on Footnotes,' *Text* 5 (1991): 86–90.

9 'Robert Fulford on Books,' *Toronto Daily Star*, 23 May 1961.

10 Dorothy Smith, 'A Peculiar Eclipsing: Women's Exclusion from Man's Culture,' *Women's Studies International Quarterly* 1 (1978): 281–95, at 287.

11 Ethel Wilson, 'Of Alan Crawley,' *Canadian Literature* 19 (1964): 33–42, at 34.

12 Quoted in George Robinson, 'Alan Crawley and Contemporary Verse,' *Canadian Literature* 41 (1969): 87–96, at 90.

13 Mary Ellmann, *Thinking about Women* (New York: Harcourt, Brace, 1968), 29.

14 Anne Wilkinson Papers, Thomas Fisher Rare Book Library, University of Toronto.

15 Anne Wilkinson Papers, Thomas Fisher Rare Book Library, University of Toronto.

16 Wilkinson, *Poetry*, 62.

17 Anne Wilkinson, *The Collected Poems of Anne Wilkinson*, ed. A.J.M. Smith (Toronto: Macmillan, 1968), 81.

18 Anne Wilkinson Papers, Thomas Fisher Rare Book Library, University of Toronto.

19 Anne Wilkinson Papers, Thomas Fisher Rare Book Library, University of Toronto.

20 'Critically Speaking,' CBC radio, 15 July 1951.

21 *Poetry of Our Time*, ed. Louis Dudek (Toronto: Macmillan, 1966), 225.

22 Wilkinson, *Collected Poems*, 3.

23 Alice Munro, *Dance of the Happy Shades* (Toronto: Ryerson, 1968), 59–74.

24 Anne Wilkinson, letter to Alan Crawley, 11 May 1949. Douglas Library Archives, Queen's University, Kingston, Ontario.

25 Sidonie Smith, *A Poetics of Women's Autobiography* (Bloomington: Indiana University Press, 1987), 53.

26 *Tamarack Review* 20 (1961): 28–52.

27 'Robert Fulford on Books.'

28 Wilkinson, *Collected Poems*, 179–207.

29 Donald H. Reiman, *Romantic Texts and Contexts* (Columbia: University of Missouri Press, 1987), 169–70.

30 Wilkinson, *Poetry*, 181.

31 Lisa Dickson, 'Anxiety and the Relational "I" in the Works of Anne Wilkinson' (unpublished paper, McMaster University, April 1994).

32 Wilkinson, *Collected Poems*, 140.

33 Quoted in a personal letter to me, July 1995.

34 Quoted in bell hooks, *Talking Back* (Toronto: between the lines, 1988), 158.

35 Anne Wilkinson Papers, Thomas Fisher Rare Book Library, University of Toronto.

36 Maxine Kumin, *To Make a Prairie*. Quoted in Carolyn G. Heilbrun, 'Non-Autobiographies of "Privileged" Women: England and America,' in *Life/Lines*, ed. Bella Brodzki and Celeste Schenck (Ithaca: Cornell University Press, 1988), 62–76, at 76.

37 Heilbrun, 'Non-Autobiographies,' at 63 and 76.

38 A recent exhibition in the Robarts Library of the University of Toronto showed old photographs of the scenes mentioned in Ondaatje's novel. One section featured Anne Wilkinson and Roches Point.

39 Katherine Acheson, 'Anne Wilkinson in Michael Ondaatje's *In the Skin of a Lion*,' *Canadian Literature* 145 (1995): 107–20, at 107 and 108.

40 Acheson, 'Anne Wilkinson,' 109, 116, 110.

41 Wilkinson, *Poetry*, 140.

NAOMI BLACK

2 'Not a novel, they said': Editing Virginia Woolf's *Three Guineas*[1]

'... my vanity reminds me, that [*Three Guineas*] is selling very well, tho' none of the shops at first would take it. Not a novel, they said, and the public won't touch anything controversial about women.'[2]

I

I was asked to prepare this paper because I am working on an edition of Virginia Woolf's *Three Guineas* for the Shakespeare Head Press Edition of Woolf, which will include all of Woolf's novels, plus *A Room of One's Own*, *Flush*, *Roger Fry* and, of course, *Three Guineas*. This edition is both scholarly and designed for the student, though for copyright reasons it will not be available in paperback at least in the short run. Our emphasis is on providing a 'good' text, one that is properly edited, annotated, and placed in context.[3] I am the only editor in the series who is not a literary scholar. In a context of literary studies, I remain a political scientist.

Therefore, when I started work on this paper, I began by thinking, why me?, or, more decorously, what do I as a particular individual bring to this particular task of editing? The answers to this question turned out to be complex, and related importantly to the nature of *Three Guineas*. As my epigraph notes, booksellers said that the book was 'not a novel,' and that 'the public' would find it 'controversial' and not buy it. In fact, the book is not a novel, and it is certainly controversial, but a substantial public continues to be willing, even eager, to buy it. This paper will therefore discuss the genre of *Three Guineas*, its public, and its message, all controversial topics because of Virginia Woolf's feminism. I shall begin with the feminism.

Why I am editing *Three Guineas* is, to some degree, serendipitous and personal. But it grows out of my interest in and my writing on feminism, on feminist theory, and therefore on Virginia Woolf and particularly *Three Guineas*. The conference for which this paper was written had the nicely ambiguous title 'Editing Women.' In my own case, it was pointed out to me, it was matter of 'Editing Feminists' – a feminist editing a feminist. It is true that 'feminists' and 'women' are the same to some extent. I have argued in the past that only women can be feminists, so that logically both the editor and the editor's subject, if feminists, have to be women.[4] And surely feminist action groups, organizations of the marginalized who are seeking to assert their autonomy, can be composed only of those needing change. For it is not possible to seek someone else's self-determination.

Feminist analysis, by contrast, can be done by anyone, but those who are not women may find it less interesting, less salient, less linked to their own experience except in some sort of imaginative identification (the iron entering into the soul of those who have not been chained, as the abolitionists said). For example, men, however sympathetic, are unlikely to react in quite the same way as women to the London Library episode that was one part of what fuelled *Three Guineas*. This little event is worth recounting, for it reflects importantly on the nature of the book it foreshadowed.

By 9 April 1935, Virginia Woolf was already taking notes for a sequel to *A Room of One's Own*, to be called, perhaps, 'On Being Despised.' She wrote in her diary 'I met Morgan [E.M. Forster] in the London Library yesterday & flew into a passion.' He said to her: 'And Virginia, you know I'm on the Co[mmittee] here ... and we've been discussing whether to allow ladies.' Woolf records her response:

> It came over me that they were going to put me on: & I was going to refuse: Oh but they do – I said. There was Mrs. Green ...

Forster then said:

> Yes yes – there was Mrs. Green. And Sir Leslie Stephen said, never again. She was so troublesome. And I said, havent ladies improved? But they were all quite determined. No no no, ladies are quite impossible. They wouldnt hear of it.

And Woolf writes, 'See how my hand trembles. I was so angry ...' The diary passage goes on to imagine that a woman friend is offered some honour usually reserved for men. It ends as follows:

> You didnt tell them what you thought of them for daring to suggest
> that you should rub your nose in that pail of offal? I remarked ...
> The veil of the temple – which, whether university or cathedral,
> was academic or ecclesiastical I forget – was to be raised, & as an
> exception she was to be allowed to enter in. But what about my
> civilisation? For 2,000 years we have done things without being paid
> for doing them. You cant bribe me now.[5]

Feminists are more likely than other women to share Virginia
Woolf's indignation, yet that episode can bring out feminist responses
in women not previously radicalized. That is, it can make them angry
at Mrs Green's having been made the stand-in for a whole class of
human beings who are seen as unfit to do what men do as a matter of
course.[6] *Three Guineas* is in effect an attempt to provoke just such an
irritated awareness of the structures of sexist exclusion. Woolf would
like, precisely, to make women conscious of the existence of 'my
civilisation' and the need to refuse any offers of joining the boys.

The nature of Woolf's feminism is crucial to an assessment of her
writing, especially in *Three Guineas*. Many women thought, when they
became women's movement activists, that the case they had to make
– what had persuaded them – was simply obvious. Once understood,
it would be accepted by everyone. However, most feminists did not
make the arguments Woolf did. Instead, they argued within the frame-
work of liberal beliefs, saying that women, if given the chance, were
as rational as men. Give women that chance, treat them fairly and edu-
cate them as well as men, and they would make their way. By contrast,
Woolf presented a deeply radical sort of feminism. In *Three Guineas*,
war is not her main target; in this her critics are correct. For her, war
is only one of the products, admittedly one of the worst products, of
a system of power and domination that has its roots in gender hierarchy. That hierarchy, and all others, are the targets of her feminism.

Woolf's radical feminism is both tough and sophisticated, and it has
transformative implications that are quite staggering. Q.D. Leavis,
possibly the most hostile critic of *Three Guineas*, understood the book
very well, saying that what Woolf wanted would be the end of civilization as we know it.[7] To which, again, the radical feminist who was
Virginia Woolf replied: And what about my civilization?

Woolf's sort of feminism is not something likely to be persuasive to
most men. But it is a feminism that I share, and that I consider importantly political – which is finally the justification for having *Three
Guineas* edited by a political scientist – who is a feminist.

II

Let us now turn to *Three Guineas* itself, looking at the sequence of texts that produced the final volume. Following that process is not easy. We do not have a full manuscript, either holograph or typed, though there are some fragments.[8] Also relevant are sections of Woolf's extensive reading notes, and the three scrapbooks in which, probably beginning in 1935, she collected material for *Three Guineas*: newspaper clippings, pamphlets, letters, photographs, appeals of various sorts, and quotations copied out from many sources – the sort of material that librarians call ephemera.[9] However, a fair amount of work has been done on the origins of *Three Guineas*, so that the list of available published sources is an extensive one. 'Published' is important from the point of view of the Shakespeare Head edition, since, for inclusion in the edition's volumes, we are limiting ourselves to published or at least type-set works.

Published, then, we have seven stages of *Three Guineas*. The book started as a talk, given on 21 January 1931, at a celebration in honour of the militant suffragette and composer Ethel Smyth, who also spoke.[10] This talk has survived in two forms: part of Woolf's longhand notes and a text that she both typed and corrected in longhand herself, as was her regular practice. Both of these documents have been transcribed and published.[11] If these two texts are considered versions one and two of the future *Three Guineas*, version three is the talk as published posthumously, in a shorter version, in a collection of Woolf's essays in 1942.[12] Virginia Woolf entitled the talk 'Professions for Women,' and Leonard Woolf used the same title for the published essay.

Almost two years after her speech (11 October 1932), Virginia Woolf began developing it into what she briefly called an essay. Within a month she had changed the title to 'novel-essay.'[13] The resulting draft alternated incomplete chapters of a projected novel with six essays on what became some of the main themes of *Three Guineas*: the impact on women of paternal power, of lack of economic independence, of limited education, and of the threat of aggressive male sexuality ('street love'). Woolf referred to the draft essays as 'interchapters.' On 2 February 1933, she recorded that she was removing the interchapters and 'compacting them in the text.' At that point, she still intended to include some scholarly apparatus with the novel, in the form of an appendix of dates, that survived only as the dates heading the different sections.[14] The text she then began working on, which took five more very difficult years to complete, became her popular, long, realistic novel *The Years*, published in 1937. Most of the factual material from the interchapters reappears in *Three Guineas*.

Woolf effectively put off writing *Three Guineas* until she was through with *The Years*. In the meantime, there were frequent references to it in her diary, and she seems to have started portions of it independently of both the interchapters and *The Years*. As early as 3 September 1931, she recorded in her diary that she had written a 'whole chapter of my Tap at the Door or whatever it is.' On 14 April 1935, she noted ruefully that she had been 'vagrant' and tried to sketch out her book on professions and made 'the interesting discovery that one cant propagate at the same time as write fiction.'[15] These fragments have not survived but the manuscript that includes the interchapters has been transcribed and published as *The Pargiters*, using the initial title of the essay-novel (it is the name of the family on which the novel centres). The aborted interchapters can therefore be considered the fourth printed version of what was to be *Three Guineas*.

Shortly before *Three Guineas* was published in book form, it was serialised in the United States: version five. 'Three USA papers' rejected it but 'Women Must Weep' appeared in two instalments in the *Atlantic Monthly* (May and June 1938).[16] This abridged version of the final text, without notes or illustrations, was carefully prepared by Woolf herself. In some places, she seems to have adapted her text for American readers. Thus, 'a Grenfell point of view, a Knebworth point of view,' became 'the soldier's and airman's point of view' and, more mundanely, 'a bunch of spillikins' became 'a box of matches.'[17] But the main constraint was surely the need to reduce the manuscript's size drastically. Bereft of the endnotes and of many of the full text's more memorable images and examples, the result is a simpler, somewhat less feminist version of the book.

The title of the serial is also of some importance, for it underlines the strong linkage of *Three Guineas* with the English women's movement, and with the anti-war strands in feminism. The second instalment of the serial has an added subtitle, so that it has become 'Women Must Weep – Or Unite against War.' The wording suggests a deliberate echo of Charles Kingsley's 'Men must work and women must weep,' in his well-known poem 'Three Fishers.' The suffrage group closest to Woolf, the National Union of Women's Suffrage Societies, had quoted Kingsley's line in 1917 to justify their stance about war. For the suffragists, Kingsley's description of women's role as one of resignation and lamentation served as a foil for their own argument that women must strive 'to understand the causes of this recurrent madness [war], so that they may heal it.'[18] This was the message that Woolf would later incorporate into *Three Guineas*; it is not to be found in *The Pargiters* although it is central to *The Years*.

Finally there is the book *Three Guineas* itself, in its two first editions, published in England in June and in the United States in August 1938 (thus making it possible to squeeze in the serial for the North American market). A computer collation has shown that the texts are almost identical.[19] These editions both include the same five photographs and 124 endnotes.[20]

The booksellers' comment that *Three Guineas* is 'not a novel' is, evidently, an understatement, for the different versions take a very wide variety of forms. The essay 'Professions for Women' retains the lecture structure and locutions as well as an identification of where the talk was given. The serial 'Women Must Weep' is in letter form. It also includes citations (with rather unspecific sources), and all later published versions of the full manuscript have the endnotes. But the photographs, which are an important addition to the text, were omitted from paperback reprints until editions from the 1990s that combined *A Room of One's Own* with *Three Guineas* in one volume.[21]

Not a novel – but what is it? *Three Guineas* is a long, complicated book that uses facts to bolster an argument, along with a form of documentation appropriate to a scholarly publication. It is also a book that has a fictionalized narrative frame and does some unusual processing of the 'facts' used. The notes, grouped at the end, make up a full fifth of the volume. They include a large number of substantial essays, and the coinage of terms like 'educated man's daughter' and 'ignorantsia,' as well as a number of passages that slyly debunk the very exercise of annotation. Woolf was somewhat disingenuous when she told Vita Sackville-West: 'all I wanted was to state a very intricate case as plainly and readable as I could.'[22]

Should we perhaps, like Leonard Woolf, simply call *Three Guineas* a 'political pamphlet'?[23] But this is a formulation that understates the scale of the book (329 pages in the first English edition, and 285 in the first American). Calling the book a 'pamphlet' also of course diminishes its importance, turning it into an ephemeral little booklet. It is true that Hogarth published a number of 'pamphlet' series that they took with the utmost seriousness, and that Woolf herself occasionally referred to *Three Guineas* as a pamphlet. But it seems clear that she thought of the book as something more substantial. When she was waiting with a certain anxiety for the first reactions to the volume, she wrote in her diary that she might 'sum it all up in 6 months in a pamphlet ...'[24] Perhaps she had in mind something like the twenty-seven-page 'Reviewers' that she published in the Hogarth Press Sixpenny Pamphlet series in November 1938, where she continued ferociously the attack on literary practices that she had sketched in *Three Guineas*.

Pamphlet or not, it does matter what the genre of the book is. As a teacher, I find it important that students recognize that these are not real letters, and this is not a real letter-writer. And surely such distinctions matter for our understanding of both the literary and the political nature of *Three Guineas*.

III

The literary form of *Three Guineas* is one familiar from English novels: epistolary. More precisely, it is framed as answers to the accumulated appeals for money and support sent to Woolf, as a well-known author and one of the few women of her time who was a public figure. Before she adopted the metaphor of the three guinea donations, one of the names she had for the work was 'Answers to Correspondents.'[25] The letters found in *Three Guineas* correspond to the argument of the book.

The first words of the book are 'Three years is a long time to leave a letter unanswered ...'[26] The book is then set up as a single letter to a specific man – the signatory of a begging letter. This device was also reflected in one of the many names used temporarily for the text. In March 1936 Woolf was thinking of calling it 'Letter to an Englishman' and doing it as a single letter: 'after all separate letters break continuity so.'[27] Throughout the book, the fictional author stresses that she is writing to a (fictional) male stranger who has taken the unusual step of asking a woman how, in her opinion, war can be prevented. More exactly, he thinks he knows the answer, and accordingly asks her to sign a manifesto about intellectual freedom, to give money to his society, and to join it. The letter-writer does finally agree to sign the manifesto and to give him some money – a guinea.

This is, it seems, a reasonable sum to give. A guinea was originally a gold coin, but by the twentieth century it had become a notional figure, equivalent to a pound plus a shilling. A slightly pretentious concept, it was the unit in which bills were submitted by professionals of the sort whom Woolf mocked in *Three Guineas*. The Hogarth dust jackets of *Three Guineas*, done by Woolf's artist sister, Vanessa Bell, showed three cheques, presumably worth a guinea each. Writing to

Bell about the dust jacket for first American edition, Woolf joked: 'and so you've killed 2 birds with 3 cheques.'[28] It has been calculated that in 1938 a guinea would have been worth just under £30 of 1990 currency, or somewhere in the neighbourhood of $60 Canadian, nearer $50 American – a substantial but not outstanding contribution.[29] Three guineas would then be something between $150 and $200.

The letter-writer does not, however, join the society, but instead recommends that women join her in a 'society of outsiders' that will be a non-organization of opposition to fascism and to the patriarchy that produces it. 'Outsiders' will become participants in public life but abjure all the dimensions of hierarchy and domination. They will pledge themselves to reject any public honours or awards offered to them, as the diary entry about the London Library foreshadows. Women will thus do their own particular best to prevent war, by countering the conditions that produce it.

The correspondent-narrator in *Three Guineas* also sends two other guineas to good causes, answering, she says, other appeals awaiting a response from her. The remaining two groups to which she gives money are a women's college and a women's organization supporting women in professions. And she states explicitly that the efforts of these groups will contribute to ending war by enabling women to transform current society.

Such arguments about women and war continue to be important for feminists. At the time of the 1991 Gulf War against Iraq, radical feminist Carol Anne Douglas wrote a piece entitled 'Dear Ms. Woolf, We Are Returning Your Guineas,' in which she lamented that Woolf's prescriptions for education were not being followed. At the beginning of the 1990s, women's integration into public life meant that they increasingly shared the 'unreal loyalties' that, according to *Three Guineas*, made men willing to go to war. As Douglas noted in something close to despair, women were even serving in the military, with support from feminist theorists and women's organizations.[30]

Woolf's arguments are presented within a far more complex epistolary structure than is usually recognized. Once they have realized that *Three Guineas* is made up of more than one letter, readers tend to think of its three chapters as corresponding to three letters, each enclosing one of the three donated guineas. In fact, no less than eleven letters or drafts of letters are mentioned or quoted from in the book. Some of these are presented as letters that the author has received and some as letters or draft letters that she writes.

First, there is the framing letter that is the book – a very odd letter, with its illustrations and endnotes, and no indication of date or place, no salutation or closing statement or signature.[31] The voice of this framing letter, as of most of the other enclosed letters, is that of a lecturer or essayist rather than a correspondent. Next there is the peace society's manifesto, which is, characteristically, in the form of a letter intended to be published in a newspaper. The manifesto is not given in full, but quoted in part. Its goal is 'to protect culture and intellectual liberty' as a way of combatting war.[32]

A third letter received by the author, presumably taking the form of an appeal for support, is not represented by text but by a description of the enclosed photographs of dead children and devastated buildings from the Spanish Civil War; the reader is told that it was sent to the author by the Spanish government in the winter of 1936–7. Given its source and timing, this letter would most probably have been about lifting the weapons embargo imposed on the various elements in the Spanish Civil War by a group of nations under British leadership, an embargo blatantly ignored by the fascists who were then destroying the Spanish republic. These reports of the disasters of war form the most powerful section of the argument in *Three Guineas* that women must seek some new way to prevent wars and the things which cause them.

Thus far, the begging letters are general appeals related to war and sent by societies or groups made up of both women and men. The remaining letters comprise two appeals from women's groups and six versions of responses to them. The first of these feminist appeals is an honorary treasurer's letter asking for money to rebuild a women's college at Cambridge; this is the fourth letter of *Three Guineas*. As a possible reply, we are given a draft letter outlining what the college should be like and a second, substitute draft telling the honorary treasurer to spend the donated money for rags, petrol, and matches to burn down the existing college; these are letters five and six. Finally, a much shorter letter gives money to the college with no conditions. Women must be educated so that they can earn their own living; otherwise they will be at home facilitating war by their ignorance and dependency. This is letter seven.

Letter eight is from another honorary treasurer, this time asking for help for needy professional women, up to and including items to sell at a bazaar and reusable, worn evening dresses and stockings. Here is one of the book's most telling examples of the plight of even middle-class women in the labour force. The appeal is, of course, not for today's fragile nylons but for sturdy woollen and cotton hose that could be darned at a time when respectable working women still did not wear trousers. The request is identified as from the London and National Society for Women's Service, the group for whom Woolf gave the lecture on professions for women and to whose library she regularly donated books and money.[33]

Letter nine is a draft letter to this second honorary treasurer, satirically saying that surely professional women are rich and powerful and, since they are, why haven't they ended war? Since such isn't the case, '"the woman's movement" has proved itself a failure.'[34] Take this guinea, to burn down the association's building; then go back to the kitchen where you belong. This second example of incendiary imagery in a pacifist book recommends violent tactics even as the author argues that women ought by upbringing to be less prone to violence than men.

Letter ten is a second-draft response to the Society for Women's Service. It is about the horrors of professional life and how women can join professions and remain uncontaminated, this last being the condition of an enclosed guinea. The final letter (number eleven) is the start of an appeal explicitly to middle-class women, urging them to sign the manifesto of the peace organization to which the cover letter of *Three Guineas* is written. The audience is then narrowed to those middle-class women who earn their living by reading and writing and, further still, to those who have enough to live on and 'read and write ... for [their] own pleasure' and are therefore able to be disinterested.[35] The narrator notes that this letter may be destined for as few as 250 women, given the limited opportunities and inferior pay available to women, and their disadvantages in respect to ownership and inheritance of property.

Woolf ends the book by saying that the letter-writer will give a guinea to her initial correspondent's campaign and she will also sign his manifesto because the causes of intellectual liberty and peace are ones which women and men can and should support together. But she will not join the society. The reasons she gives make Woolf's sort of feminism very clear:

> Different we are, as facts have proved, both in sex and in education. And it is from that difference, as we have already said, that our help can come, if help we can, to protect liberty, to prevent war. But if we sign this form which implies a promise to become active members of

your society, it would seem that we must lose that difference and therefore sacrifice that help.[36]

IV

Three Guineas is neither one nor three nor eleven actual letters, then, but it could still be thought of as responses by Virginia Woolf to actual appeals made to her. This is probably a mistake. To begin with, we should distinguish between Virginia Woolf and the fictional letter-writer. In *A Room of One's Own*, the imaginary author is individualized to the point of an imaginary name, an imaginary aunt, and imaginary employment as a governess and a maker of artificial flowers. In *Three Guineas*, the fictionalized narrator is less clearly delineated, but she is still not Virginia Woolf. In fact, Woolf herself had often been asked by men to participate in efforts to bring about peace or intellectual liberty.[37] When she was asked – also frequently – to further feminist endeavours, she did not respond with the occasional frivolity that lightens the tone of *Three Guineas*. We have many actual examples of her correspondence with feminist activists, and in them her anger is real and unmediated.

Nor should we think of the central letters of *Three Guineas* as addressed to particular people or organizations. This may seem obvious, but critics continue to make such assumptions. Thus, Christine Froula nominates as the first, main interlocutor of *Three Guineas* the distinguished peace activist Robert, Viscount Cecil of Chelwood, President of the League of Nations Union and a Nobel Peace Laureate in 1937, signatory to a leaflet from the International Peace Campaign.[38] But Viscount Cecil and his wife, Nellie, were long-time friends of Leonard and Virginia Woolf. She hardly had to imagine him as some unknown barrister. And if Maynard Keynes's interest in pig-breeding seems to have supplied one feature of the imaginary correspondent's character, Keynes bore no other resemblance to the family man sketched out at the opening of *Three Guineas*.

In fact, as might be expected, Woolf reworked rather than simply reproduced the appeals that she used as an organizing device for *Three Guineas*. For example, an early letter from the International Peace Campaign asks for support and a signature on a Manifesto that Woolf labelled 'War and Writers' when she stuck it into her scrapbook.[39] The source of this appeal sounds like a plausible candidate for the society to which Woolf was writing the framing document of *Three Guineas*.

However, the peace society's letter is in fact signed by 'Dame Adelaide Livingstone.' So much for the repeated comments in *Three Guineas* about how unusual it is for men to ask women what to do about war.

It is perhaps unnecessary to note that the appeals referred to, when real, had not remained unanswered. Nor were Woolf's responses what *Three Guineas* suggests. Thus she explicitly identifies and cites an appeal from a professional women's group (the London and National Society for Women's Service) that asked her for bazaar donations.[40] We know that she had in fact become a member of that group in 1932, and had herself solicited support for its library and attempted to sell the manuscript of *A Room of One's Own* on its behalf; she would not have had to fantasize as she does about the writer of the appeal.[41] For that matter, even the (imaginary) letter-writer could not really expect the recipients of her letters to do what she suggests: to burn down colleges, to wind up the women's movement as a failure, or even, more moderately, to take a pledge of chastity, even intellectual chastity, or to refuse all honours.

We can nevertheless note with interest how the literary device of the letter form works. To begin with, it always incorporates a correspondent – an assumption about the nature of the person who is being addressed. The letter is 'a transitive form,' with 'an objectified reader inside.'[42] For the frame letter of *Three Guineas*, the recipient is specified as a barrister who has had some success in the world. But is he really the intended recipient of the 'letter'? That is, should we think of Woolf as writing, if not to a particular individual, at least to some larger group of professional men like the imaginary correspondent? Analysts of *Three Guineas* have, in fact, tended to make that mistaken assumption, and to express concern that the tone or the arguments of the book are ill-suited for such an audience.

The letter, so very much a women's medium, has two possible functions that are relevant here.[43] First of all, it does in general provide a way in which to speak bluntly, as one might not face-to-face, to someone who may be hostile but nevertheless potentially open to persuasion. Because the fictional letters include money, the (fictional) recipients would read to the end and perhaps make some gesture of agreement (though is one guinea enough for that?). This is not the only place where, often more explicitly, Woolf urges women to use what economic leverage they have. We could notice also that Woolf seems to recommend the use of cover letters for donations as a means of influencing not just male peace activists or politicians, but also the women who run colleges for women and associations supporting women in the professions. But after all, since the guineas are fictional, we are not talking about a real audience, whether male or female.

At the same time, those women represented by fictional honorary treasurers of women's organizations are, I believe, part of the intended actual audience of the real book. Another part is the similar middle-class women, not yet converted to feminism, who might be persuaded by the documentation provided, and who might also respond to the tone of the book. Woolf was much relieved by the enthusiastic response to *Three Guineas* from her friend Philippa Strachey, Secretary of the London and National Society for Women's Service. 'It is what we have panted for for years and years,' wrote that long-time suffra-gist and feminist activist.[44] It seems that the occasionally comic man of good will who is the ostensible recipient of the letter is merely a literary device, and the letter is aimed at quite another group – women like Pippa Strachey or potentially like her, women who were feminist activists or might become such.

Here we move to another important characteristic of letters. As historians have come to realize that the letter is a classic way for women to communicate privately among themselves. *Three Guineas*, then, seems to represent something of a paradox, for printing 23,750 copies of a published letter is the opposite of private, and certainly Hogarth made serious efforts to get booksellers to stock the book.[45] But if we see the intended recipient as plural – all the women who might be supportive of Woolf's version of feminism – then circulation is more to the point than privacy. And perhaps the readers can after all count on privacy to some degree, since it is not to be expected that men like the fictional correspondent would want to read the book (which in the real world does not hand out guineas to them, but instead costs seven shillings and sixpence). That many men would read the book was un-likely, anyway, given what we know about how men have responded to the subject and to the tone of the book. Take Quentin Bell, who found *Three Guineas* so infuriating that he felt obliged to refute it repeatedly, even in a memoir written in his patriarchal eighties.[46] It seems unlikely that he would have read it when he was a young socialist hoping for a United Front – if it had not been written by his aunt! It was probably men rather than women whom the booksellers had in mind when they said that the public did not want to read anything controversial about women.

Let us look for a moment at the tone of *Three Guineas*. It has been variously described. Woolf's dear but non-feminist friend Vita Sackville-West found it charming but unpersuasive, while Quentin Bell was only one of many to be enraged by it. Some feminist critics find it insufficiently angry.[47] Woolf herself wrote in letters both that she had had to 'secrete a jelly to slip quotations down people's throats' and that the book was intended to make people angry and to say irritating things.[48] It is perhaps best described as deliberately teasing. I was told by a friend who had been a member of New York Radical Feminists that the tone of *Three Guineas* reminded her of the provocative way in which she and her group had phrased public statements in the late 1960s. The target of the hostile response directed at radical feminists including Virginia Woolf is not the style or the speaker, but what is said. But those who are receptive to the message may also respond positively to the tone.

Who is she, the speaker or writer of *Three Guineas*, the first person of the relationship that defines a letter? She is an 'educated man's daughter' – Woolf's phrase for women like herself, who in her view should not be labelled 'bourgeois,' because they lacked the capital and the environment of their fathers' and brothers' class.[49] The voice in the book is the voice of the daughters of educated men talking to one another, and they laugh – at men – as they work up their indignation together. They are elite women, with less power than their elite brothers, but nevertheless with the potential to produce large-scale social change, even an end to war and to its source, sexism.

Perhaps we should think of *Three Guineas* as a fundraising appeal and programme for middle-class women's activism. This activism is directed against all the senior professions including the government and especially established religion, all public ceremonies and hierarchy. It is also directed against militarism and war. Its positive goals include educational reform, transformation of the media, entry of women into all professions and occupations, equal pay and benefits for women, and a women's movement that includes peace activism and war resistance.

As the author of *Three Guineas*, Virginia Woolf is best considered an essayist rather than a novelist. In addition, she is a professional literary journalist who knows that raw facts must be processed if the result is to be published and read. It is important to remember Woolf's continuing experience with magazines and newspapers, including some produced by and for women. We can assume she knows her likely audience, and what they will find acceptable. How could she be so naive as to think, for example, that her brother-in-law Clive Bell would find the illustrations in *Three Guineas*, let alone the arguments, either comic or telling? He had been a hunting, shooting man, after all, even though he was a pacifist.

V

Three Guineas has two unique problems for an editor of the works of Virginia Woolf: the notes and the illustrations. I shall put aside the notes for consideration in another place and continue the emphasis of the lecture-cum-slideshow on which this paper is based.

What exactly is the significance of the five unidentified photographs that Woolf provided in *Three Guineas*? They are surely important, for she mentions her intention of including them as early as 16 February 1932. Musing on the possible title of 'Men are like that' ('no thats too patently feminist') she reflects that she has 'collected enough powder to blow up St Pauls' and adds 'it is to have 4 pictures.'[50] The pictures, it seems, are part of the explosive mixture, and they are conspicuous in the scrapbooks she is keeping.

We all often include photographs in a letter, though if we remember we give them more identification than Woolf's simple descriptive phrases in *Three Guineas*: 'A General,' 'Heralds,' 'A University Procession,' 'A Judge,' 'An Archbishop.' These are not the familiar family photographs of Bloomsbury: Virginia Woolf smoking and squinting against the sun, Lytton Strachey sprawled bonelessly in a deckchair, the Bell children running around with no clothes on. But these photographs are nevertheless real pictures of real events, clipped from English newspapers in the 1930s.

One of my problems as an editor is to identify the individual people and occasions of the photographs.[51] However, the pictures' actual subjects are immaterial to their purpose. And in this the photographs differ drastically from the personal or propaganda photographs that they look like. It usually matters who was in that family photograph and when; it matters even more that the horrors of Spain are from a specific time and place. By deliberate contrast, the photographs in *Three Guineas* are anonymous. In an ostentatiously documented book, no sources are given for the pictures. Their impersonal titles make the initial point that the photographs are, as it were, generic – the very model of a general and so forth. The illustrations to *Three Guineas* thus imply a structural analysis of the situation of men – and by implication, women – in contemporary society.

Looked at in isolation from the text of *Three Guineas*, in fact, these pictures are unremarkable. It is true that they are all photographs of men, but they are of public events in which women are relatively infrequently found. Even today, women are not often generals, heralds, judges, or university chancellors, and there has still not been a woman

A general (reproduced by permission of The Society of Authors).

Heralds (reproduced by permission of The Society of Authors).

archbishop. That is, of course, the second point being made: the absence of women from the formal, ceremonial contexts that attest to public power.

A third and major point made by the photographs, but only when they are placed in the context of the arguments of *Three Guineas*, is that men are vain, and arrogant, and besotted with status. The pictures are notable for the display of gorgeous apparel, every piece of which has meaning and indicates rank and power. This dimension is what made some male readers apoplectic, including Bloomsbury men whom we might have expected not to care. However, I can well believe that, like myself, the intended women readers laughed.

Woolf used photographs surprisingly often in her books. There are four photographs among the eight illustrations to *Orlando*. Those photographs, like the ones in *Three Guineas*, lose their satiric impact unless combined with the text. That book is in part a joke, as is *Flush*, which also has five photographs including one in which the Woolfs' cocker spaniel sits in for Elizabeth Barrett Browning's dog. The photographs in the biography *Roger Fry* are all straightforward pictures of

A university procession (reproduced by permission of The Society of Authors).

people and places.[52] The photographs of *Three Guineas* are not jokes but neither are they simply illustrations. Their meaning comes from their context and from the intention of the person who supplied them.

The nature of the photographs in *Three Guineas* can best be demonstrated by considering some other, somewhat similar photographs. We can begin with pictures taken by Virginia Woolf's great-aunt, Julia Margaret Cameron, a pioneering Victorian photographer with a continuing reputation today.[53] In 1926, Woolf put together a collection of Cameron's work, along with an introduction by herself and a critical essay by Roger Fry. The title of the volume was *Victorian Photographs of Famous Men and Fair Women*.[54] 'Famous men and fair women' – it summarizes the society that Woolf was to attack in *Three Guineas*. There can be no doubt that Mrs. Cameron's beautiful, static photographs were meant admiringly. For example, she made several formal portraits of Benjamin Jowett, Master of Balliol College and Regius Professor of Greek at Oxford. But today Jowett's elaborate white tie, his self-satisfied expression, and the book spread open in his hands add up to something that could easily be 'A Professor' for *Three Guineas*.

A judge (reproduced by permission of The Society of Authors).

A related but slightly different point is made by Mrs Cameron's much-praised illustrations for Tennyson's *Idylls of the King*. Tennyson liked the series very much, and so did the photographer. Even with context, however, these posed tableaux look ridiculous to us today, as we wince or giggle at the fur rugs draped as cloaks and the coalscuttle helmet that looms over Mr Cameron's Victorian beard. These photographs suggest something about taste and style, and about temporal setting. By contrast, it is remarkable that the figures in the *Three Guineas* photos do *not* look dated almost sixty years after their publication. Nor are the statements they make, once they are inserted in the text.

Moving away from Mrs Cameron's work, we can consider an English photograph from the inter-war years that at first glance seems ideally designed to serve as an additional illustration to *Three Guineas*, perhaps entitled A Lord Chancellor. Once more, an elderly man dressed in elaborate robes and wig, his fur cape held up by an attendant, marches in a formal public procession, watched by an admiring crowd, preceded by a mace and other regalia. Lord Chancellor Sankey,

An archbishop (reproduced by permission of The Society of Authors).

of His Majesty's Privy Council, at Temple Bar, 1929, is on his way to deliver a legal judgment. But as it happens, he is about to affirm the status of Canadian women as 'persons' under the British North America Act, at a time when the highest court of appeal for the Dominion of Canada is the Judicial Committee of the Privy Council. The image thus represents, not the patriarchal figure of 'A Lord Chancellor' but an early triumph of the Canadian women's movement. In fact, I encountered the photograph as the frontispiece of a postwar book on woman suffrage in Canada.[55] The Lord Chancellor was presented there as a symbol of feminism's success, and of a commitment to using the existing social structures to produce a change in the situation of women. By contrast, although the text of *Three Guineas* certainly endorses the use of existing social structures to change society – why else promote women's education and their entry into the professions? – the book's photographs are used to mock the regalia of male dominance, not to celebrate women's use of the machinery of public power.

We may further amplify the context for Woolf's condemnation of male ceremonial regalia by considering photographs of an annual congress of the Women's Co-operative Guild. These pictures are to be found in *Life As We Have Known It*, a collection of memoirs and (again) letters from co-operative working class women for which Woolf wrote in 1931 another public letter to serve as the introduction to the volume.[56] Behind the stage loaded with the dignified leaders of the Guild hang an assortment of beautiful hand-sewn banners. The women's movement has never scorned pageantry, and the one Woolf knew used it deliberately; there were many gorgeous suffrage banners in the parades we have vaguely heard of. Such banners, like those of the co-operative women, are not ridiculous like those in the processions of *Three Guineas*. Made for the occasion, rather than relics of feudalism, they are contemporary and unritualized. Instead of reflecting hierarchy and male domination, they speak of hopes for a better future: peace and liberty, as sought by women.

But we should note also that, unlike the *Three Guineas* photographs, the change of times makes the co-operative women's banners look old-fashioned, even tacky. We do our pageantry differently today, aiming less at glamour and more at the demonstration of women's craft traditions as in Judy Chicago's *Dinner Party* and the many popular examples of ceremonial quilts.[57]

Finally, it is worth examining the four photographs that Leonard Woolf used for *his* anti-war book, *Quack, Quack!*, published in 1935, three years before *Three Guineas*. Two photographs described as 'Effigy of the War-God Kukailimoku from the Hawaiian Islands' (British Museum) are interleaved with 'Herr Hitler' and 'Signor Mussolini' so that the masks face the dictators side-by-side for the reader of the book. War-gods and fascist dictators match one another in vicious and slightly comic rage.

Leonard Woolf used the photographs to illustrate 'the reversion from intelligence and civilization to primitive instincts and passions' that, in his view, fascism represented in the inter-war period.[58] This was not his wife's interpretation of politics in the 1930s. For her, in *Three Guineas* and elsewhere, Hitler and Mussolini represented the extreme of that sexism and hierarchy that she thought was characteristic of men's civilization. Furthermore, the photographs in *Quack, Quack!* seem to be rather differently selected and used than those in *Three Guineas*. It is difficult to evaluate them so many years later, but if the Hitler photograph seems a hostile choice, the picture of Mussolini is relatively typical. The juxtapositions are what make the point – a condemnation by resemblance. The polemical point is obvious even without the text, although the text spells out the implications to make them clearer.

It is worth noting how Leonard Woolf's photographic satire has been undercut since 1935. A man like him would be wary today of the Eurocentrism of such a comparison. In addition, although the wars of the Hawaiians, as reported by the Europeans, were notoriously bloody, more recent anthropological analyses have demonstrated a high degree of social structuring in them. For example, a 1965 discussion of ancient Hawaiian warfare describes it as 'the warfare of feudalism, with its recognized rules and formalities, its prayers, invocations, and ceremonial preparation,' concluding that Hawaiian warfare itself was 'highly developed and ... far removed from savagery in its conduct and regulations.'[59] But Virginia Woolf's description of 'modern' male ritual and hierarchy seems more rather than less accurate sixty years after it was first published, while her laments, criticisms, and recommendations for change remain fresh and relevant.

VI

When I was reading the published 'Professions for Women' in Woolf's collected essays, I strayed into the previous essay, which I did not know, entitled 'Why?' Woolf was asked to write it for a journal called *Lysistrata* produced by students of Somerville College, one of the women's colleges at Oxford.[60] The essay was first published in May

1934, and I read it with some amazement; it can serve as summary of the enduring interest of *Three Guineas*.

'Why?' begins with a statement – ironic – of Woolf's disappointment that *Lysistrata* is well printed and looks prosperous: 'As I turned the pages, it seemed to me that wealth must have descended upon Somerville.' She was therefore about to refuse to write for it, but to her 'relief' found that one of the writers was 'badly dressed' and that 'the women's colleges still lack[ed] power and prestige.' So here, perhaps, she could pose some of the questions that cannot be posed in places that are rich and prestigious.

'Are not women's colleges poor and young?' she asks rhetorically. 'Are they not inventive, adventurous? Are they not out to create a new——' But Woolf then notes that 'The editor forbids feminism.' Of course the question then arises, 'What is feminism?' But she says that 2000 words is not enough to answer such a question. And she finally settles for dealing with a few of 'the simplest, tamest, and most obvious' questions, such as, 'why lecture, why be lectured?'[61]

The essay 'Why?' is a useful reminder that Woolf took very seriously indeed both feminism and the potential for a feminist education and scholarship, however much she mocked them. Slight and light-hearted, 'Why?' nevertheless touches on many of the central themes of *Three Guineas*: women's education, women's poverty and lack of power, the transformational potential of feminism.

This brief reference to 'Why?' underlines the important point that *Three Guineas*, in all its incarnations, is not an isolated polemic, not just the 'sequel' to *A Room of One's Own* that even Virginia Woolf herself called it on occasion. It is, rather, a coherent presentation of the feminist beliefs about women and society that run through all of Woolf's writing and all her life.

This is why I am editing it.

NOTES

1   Since, like *Three Guineas*, this paper was first prepared and presented as a lecture, I have stayed close to lecture style and format. Like Virginia Woolf, I have amplified and added notes.

2   From a letter to Ethel Smyth, 26 June 1938. Virginia Woolf, *The Letters*, ed. Nigel Nicolson and Joanne Trautmann, 6 volumes (London: The Hogarth Press, 1975–1980), 6: 247.

3   Shakespeare Head is an imprint of Basil Blackwell in Oxford. At the

start of 1997, as I write, the Shakespeare Head Edition of Virginia Woolf has the following volumes in print: *To the Lighthouse* (edited by Susan Dick), *The Waves* (edited by James Haule and Philip Smith), *Night and Day* (edited by J.H. Stape), *Roger Fry* (edited by Diane Gillespie), *The Voyage Out* (edited by Laurence and Ruth Miller), and *Mrs Dalloway* (edited by Morris Beja). The following are in press: *Flush* (edited by Elizabeth Steele) and *Orlando* (edited by J.H. Stape).

4   Naomi Black, *Social Feminism* (Ithaca: Cornell University Press, 1989).

5   Virginia Woolf, *The Diary of Virginia Woolf*, ed. Anne Olivier Bell with Andrew McNeillie, 5 volumes (London: The Hogarth Press, 1975–1982), 4: 297–8.

6   We have only Virginia Woolf's report of Forster's claim that there was a policy against appointing more women to the committee. Perhaps Forster was being mischievous: it seems unlikely that Leslie Stephen would have taken such a position, for he was supportive of women's education and their professional activity even though he opposed any immediate grant of the vote. See Noel Annan, *Leslie Stephen: The Godless Victorian* (London: Weidenfeld and Nicolson, 1984), 109, 110, 293–4; also Leslie Stephen, *Selected Letters,* ed. John W. Bicknell, 2 volumes (London: Macmillan, 1996), 1: 103 and 213–15. Alice Stopford Green (1847–1919) was a distinguished historian and good friend of Leslie Stephen. Stephen became chair of the London Library committee in 1892; Green was elected to it in 1894 and re-elected every four years until 1916. In 1900 Stephen edited the letters of Green's deceased husband, the eminent historian J.R. Green (see Bicknell's biographical comments in his edition of the *Letters* 1: 270–2). See also Stephen's letter to his wife (*Letters* 2: 413–14 and n1); his letter of sympathy to Mrs Green on the death of her friend Mary Kingsley (*Letters* 2: 507–8); and his last, affectionate letter to Mrs Green shortly before his death (*Letters* 2: 543). Professor Eileen Power was elected to the London Library committee in 1937; in 1940 Woolf had the pleasure of refusing an offer by Forster to propose her for the committee (see Woolf, *Diary,* 5: 337).

7   'Caterpillars of the Commonwealth, Unite!' *Scrutiny* 7 (September 1938): 203–14.

8   The Berg collection of the New York Public Library has a total of 222 pages of fragmentary material, including 90 pages of holograph and 49 pages of corrected typescript, but it is not known if any of this corresponds to the 'manuscript' that was sold to 'Miss Jones' on behalf of the 'Refugees society,' at the request of May Sarton (see Woolf, *Letters*, 6: 314, 319). Hermione Lee identifies the beneficiary as

the American Guild for Cultural Freedom but perpetuates the assumption that the complete manuscript is to be found in the Berg. Hermione Lee, *Virginia Woolf* (London: Chatto and Windus, 1996), 687, n59.

9   I will not discuss these miscellaneous sources here. The crucial notebooks and scrapbooks are not difficult to work with, because Virginia Woolf herself indexed and re-indexed the material with great care, Brenda Silver has done an invaluable analysis of them, and they are available on microfilm. See Brenda R. Silver, *Virginia Woolf's Reading Notebooks* (Princeton: Princeton University Press, 1983); and her '*Three Guineas* Before and After: Further Answers to Correspondents,' in *Virginia Woolf: A Feminist Slant*, ed. Jane Marcus (Lincoln: University of Nebraska Press, 1983), 254–76.

10   It was organized by the Junior Council of the London and National Society for Women's Service, one of the descendants of the National Union of Women's Suffrage Societies. Vera Brittain, who was present at the talk, discusses the event in 'A Woman's Notebook,' *The Nation* (31 January 1931): 571, as cited in Virginia Woolf, *The Pargiters*, ed. Mitchell A. Leaska (London: The Hogarth Press, 1978), xxxv.

11   See Woolf, *The Pargiters*, ed. Leaska, xxvii–xliv, 163–7. There is some evidence that the transcription is not entirely reliable. Alex Zwerdling has shown a significant mis-transcription of Woolf's longhand corrections to the typed lecture: *Virginia Woolf and the Real World* (Berkeley: University of California Press, 1986), 348, n18.

12   Virginia Woolf, *The Death of the Moth and Other Essays* (London: The Hogarth Press, 1942).

13   Woolf, *Diary*, 4: 129.

14   Woolf, *The Pargiters*, ed. Leaska, xvi–xvii.

15   Woolf, *Diary*, 4: 300.

16   Woolf, *Diary*, 5: 130. Virginia Woolf, 'Women Must Weep,' *The Atlantic Monthly* 161 (May 1938): 585–94 and 161 (June 1938): 750–9.

17   Woolf, 'Women Must Weep,' 587.

18   Cited from the *International Women's News* in Arnold Whittick, *Woman Into Citizen* (London: Atheneum with Frederick Muller, 1979), 296.

19   Philip and Elisabeth Smith did this collation for me with their usual comforting expertise; I appreciate their help, and also the continuing assistance of James Haule.

20   The photographs are placed slightly differently in the two editions but they are in the same order; the endnotes are virtually identical except for pagination. Both editions also have two informational footnotes inserted with asterisks at the bottom of the page: the date of the

Spanish government's material being discussed (1936–7) and the ascension of Prime Minister Baldwin to Earldom (in the text, he was cited from a period before that event).

21 Virginia Woolf, *A Room of One's Own and Three Guineas*, ed. Morag Shiach (Oxford and New York: Oxford University Press, 1992); and ed. Michèle Barrett (Harmondsworth: Penguin, 1993).

22 Woolf, *Letters*, 6: 243.

23 Leonard Woolf, *Downhill All the Way: An Autobiography of the Years 1919–1939* (London: The Hogarth Press, 1967), 27.

24 Woolf, *Diary*, 5: 146.

25 Woolf, *Diary*, 5: 3.

26 Quotations from *Three Guineas* are from the first English edition (London: The Hogarth Press, 1938).

27 Woolf, *Diary*, 5: 18.

28 Woolf, *Letters*, 6: 251.

29 Jonathan Gathorne-Hardy, *The Interior Castle. A Life of Gerald Brenan* (London: Sinclair-Stevenson, 1992), 611.

30 Carol Anne Douglas: 'Commentary,' *off our backs* 21 (February 1991): 5.

31 Woolf's real-life private letters tended to be casual about date and place, but even they included addresses, salutations, conclusions, signatures; her professional letters were business-like and complete.

32 Woolf, *Three Guineas*, 154.

33 For a discussion of Woolf's relationship to various women's groups including the London and National Society for Women's Service, see my 'Virginia Woolf and the Women's Movement,' in *Virginia Woolf: A Feminist Slant*, ed. Marcus, 180–97.

34 Woolf, *Three Guineas*, 80.

35 Woolf, *Three Guineas*, 168.

36 Woolf, *Three Guineas*, 188.

37 For instance, in a letter to Ethel Smyth dated 5 March 1937, she laments, 'Why does everyone bother me about politics. Six letters to sign daily – or nearly so.' In this case, she is referring particularly to a request to put her name on a petition, along with J.D. Beresford, Somerset Maugham, Hugh Walpole, and H.G. Wells; the subject is setting up expert international commissions to enquire into the economic and structural causes of war (Woolf, *Letters*, 6: 112). See Lee, *Virginia Woolf*, 686–7 for Woolf's involvement (by invitation) in male-organized left-wing antifascism during the 1930s.

38 Froula suggests that in *Three Guineas* Virginia Woolf is responding to three specific documents preserved in her scrapbooks: 'a leaflet from

the "International Peace Campaign," signed "Cecil/The Viscount Cecil," ... a letter of 19 February 1936 from J.P. Strachey requesting that Woolf become a "Patron" of Newnham College to help launch a funding campaign ... and a flyer dated February 1936 from the National Council for Equal Citizenship ("a direct descendant of the National Union of Women's Suffrage Societies"), Dame M. Fawcett, President ...' Christine Froula, 'St. Virginia's Epistle to an English Gentleman; or, Sex, Violence, and the Public Sphere in Woolf's *Three Guineas*,' *Tulsa Studies in Women's Literature* 13 (Spring 1994): 27–56, at 50, n7. Lee, *Virginia Woolf*, 691 states authoritatively that the model for the peace society was the group 'For Intellectual Liberty' founded by, among others, Leonard Woolf. The key phrase of its 1936 recruitment pamphlet was 'the defence of culture and intellectual liberty.'

39 Silver, *Reading Notebooks*, 284 (numbers 37 and 38).

40 Woolf, *Three Guineas*, 285, n1.

41 Lee, *Virginia Woolf*, 602. We also know that Woolf wrote, in response to the Newnham College appeal, not to any honorary treasurer, but to the Principal of Newnham, her old friend Pernel Strachey, with a straightforward agreement to be a Patron of the college. Woolf, *Letters*, 6: 15. Her letter indicates that a formal response had also gone to Pernel.

42 S.P. Rosenbaum, 'Bloomsbury Letters,' in *Aspects of Bloomsbury* (London and New York: Macmillan and St. Martin's, 1998), 33.

43 Frank and Anita Kermode, introducing *The Oxford Book of Letters* (Oxford: Oxford University Press, 1995), comment, 'One conclusion rather hard to escape is that a great many of the most accomplished letter writers have been women' (xxi). Oddly, they attribute this achievement to the supposed fact that women 'have, historically, had less occasion to write merely performative letters, letters which command, promise, or threaten, so that they can afford to be more interested in themselves than in the achievement of any practical purpose unrelated to the pleasure of writing, and the pleasure of giving pleasure' (xxii). They footnote Virginia Woolf's remarks that letter-writing was 'an occupation one could carry on at odd moments ... anonymously as it were' (Virginia Woolf, 'Dorothy Osborne's Letters,' in *The Essays of Virginia Woolf*, ed. Andrew McNeillie, 4 volumes [London: The Hogarth Press, 1986–1994], 4: 554).

44 Woolf, *Diary*, 5: 147, n17.

45 16,250 copies for the United Kingdom and 7,500 for the United States. B.J. Kirkpatrick, *A Bibliography of Virginia Woolf*, 3rd edition (Oxford: Clarendon Press, 1980), 66.

46 Quentin Bell, *Elders and Betters* (London: John Murray, 1995), 212–20.

47 See Brenda Silver, 'The Authority of Anger: *Three Guineas* as Case Study,' *Signs* 16 (1991): 340–70. See also the interesting discussion of the strategic use of angry rhetoric by feminists, Barbara Tomlinson, 'The Politics of Textual Vehemence, or Go to Your Room Until You Learn How to Act,' *Signs* 22 (1996): 86–114. The echo of *A Room of One's Own* does not seem to be accidental.

48 See Woolf's letters to Vita Sackville-West, Margaret Llewelyn Davies, and her niece Philippa Woolf (aged 15) in Woolf, *Letters*, 6: 242, 251, 360.

49 Woolf, *Three Guineas*, 265, n2.

50 Woolf, *Diary*, 4: 77.

51 The endnotes also present a major challenge to the editor, for the references are often obscure and sometimes inaccurate.

52 There are either twelve or thirteen pictures, depending on the edition.

53 See *Annals of My Glass House*, photographs by Julia Margaret Cameron, text by Violet Hamilton (Seattle: Ruth Chandler Williamson Gallery, Scripps College, and University of Washington Press, 1996).

54 Julia Margaret Cameron, *Victorian Photographs of Famous Men and Fair Women*, with an introduction by Virginia Woolf and Roger Fry (London: The Hogarth Press, 1926).

55 Catherine L. Cleverdon, *The Woman Suffrage Movement in Canada*, 2nd edition (Toronto: University of Toronto Press, 1974), frontispiece. At issue was women's inclusion as 'persons' eligible to be appointed to the Canadian Senate; the conservative Supreme Court of Canada was over-ruled in 1929 by the Judicial Committee of the Privy Council.

56 *Life As We Have Known It*, ed. Margaret Llewelyn Davies with an introductory letter by Virginia Woolf (London: The Hogarth Press, 1931), frontispiece.

57 Judy Chicago, *The Dinner Party* (Harmondsworth: Penguin, 1996).

58 Leonard Woolf, *Quack, Quack!* (London: The Hogarth Press, 1935), 44.

59 Kenneth P. Emory, 'Warfare,' in *Ancient Hawaiian Civilization*, ed. Handy Craighill and Kenneth P. Emory (Rutland, VT: Charles E. Tuttle Co, 1965), 240. I should thank Jacqueline Vukman for this material on Hawaiian warfare.

60 Woolf, 'Why?' in *Collected Essays*, ed. Leonard Woolf, 4 volumes (London: The Hogarth Press, 1966–7), 2: 278–83.

61 Woolf, 'Why?' 2: 278–9.

3 Editing Lady Mary Wortley Montagu

This paper is dedicated to the memory of David Fleeman, who died in 1994. He taught me bibliography in 1966–7, the first year of his Oxford teaching career. David Fairer rightly calls him 'the leading British Johnson scholar.'[1] This makes a thread of relevance to the question of editing women: Johnson was good at getting women into print. More centrally, Fleeman was a leader of the new school of editing. Fairer mentions 'his keen awareness that a literary text is a flux upon which any printed edition is bound to impose an artificial fixity,' his 'healthy awareness of textual pragmatics,' his suspicion 'of tidy impositions of consistency upon a text that may reflect its author's uncertainties or oversights.' Fleeman himself called a text 'not a single entity but ... rather a process. Its witnesses are merely markers on the continuum of that process.' His latest work, on the nineteenth-century afterlife of Johnson's texts, led him to recognize 'la sociologie du texte': the reading of cultural attitudes through the way a period treats its texts.[2]

These ideas underlie this paper, which is in two parts. The first will briefly describe my own editorial relationship with Lady Mary Wortley Montagu; the second will trace her texts through the processes mediated by their various editors, scavengers, and custodians. Both stories will raise a question which I believe to be worth raising about any edition: as whom is the author being constructed? The second story exemplifies the especial degree of contingency which the female condition has historically imposed on women's texts above and beyond the inevitable contingency which all texts share.

This all began for me when I worked as full-time research assistant on Robert Halsband's edition of Lady Mary's *Complete Letters*.[3] Letters were a good place for me to start, because letters are of all texts perhaps the most resistant to tidying. Their susceptibility to flux is different in kind, though not in degree, from that of other texts. Our editorial principles in those days followed rules which were simple, if somewhat paradoxical, and which kept us vividly aware of the way the passage from handwriting to print inevitably imposes a regularity and uniformity which the original never knew.

When following our best text, Lady Mary's holograph, we stayed as close to it as we felt we could. But we freely made certain classes of minor modification in the interests of easy reading. Her spelling and capitalization were sacrosanct, even though they are inconsistent; and even though when we decided that any initial letter was *either* capital *or* lower-case (note the term from printing) we were unavoidably imposing a false dichotomy on her handwritten initial letters, which range smoothly upwards from uniform-with-other-letters through slightly enlarged, all the way to hugely enlarged. We expanded her *standard* abbreviations (like the ampersand, and *ye* for the, and *wn* for when) as a matter of course. We altered (that is, normally, we supplemented) her punctuation and paragraphing when we thought them, or the lack of them, likely to baffle or irritate the reader. Against the school of thought which holds that original punctuation ought to be retained for the purpose of tracing punctuation history, we would argue that these were familiar letters: their original readers knew their writer. What was right for them cannot be right for readers today.

In making such changes we were only carrying out a *version* of what any eighteenth-century printer would have done. (Of course they would have chosen different supplementary punctuation.) But when we had no manuscript, and had to follow a printed text, we followed it exactly, even though no printed text of Lady Mary's letters has the least authority, and all differ widely from her manuscripts. This scholarly convention has sound reasons: any alteration would rest on nothing but guess-work, albeit informed guess-work. Any alteration to a printed text (except the correction of unmistakable error) *might* be another step away from the original manuscript. All this was by the book in those palmy days of eighteenth-century editing. We were then seeking to make Lady Mary canonical, and today it is necessary to remember that at that date the canon had been expanding. Recent or ongoing major editions included Boswell, Burney, and Walpole as well as Pope and Johnson.

For editors of familiar letters, the manuscript is not only the original; it is also the only authentic text. These material relics are the bodies of singular and particular acts of communication, written at a particular moment and also *to* the moment in at least something of the manner of Richardson's fictional letters: at first reading they served an immediate purpose, carried a peculiar meaning, which they can never do again. The size of paper, manner of folding it, spacing of the written words, the address and seal (if any) are all intentional parts of that communication, just as poor handwriting or spelling are unintentional parts of it; any printed text belongs to a different, secondary, imitative genre. The editor of letters needs a particular reverence for the contingent and the unperfected.

After working on Montagu's letters, I edited her verse for my doctorate.[4] The proportion of her poems with holograph authority is almost as high as that of her letters (about 84 per cent), but a holograph copy of a poem generally lacks the obvious, unique authority of an original letter. Poems can be revised or they can be misremembered. Several holographs of the same poem may in some cases differ widely, and published texts or other people's copies may have as good authority as holograph. Where editions of letters to some extent imitate the original manuscripts, editions of poetry relate, by and large, only to the print medium. Nevertheless, more or less the same practices (with slightly more or less intervention) have served for Montagu's various writings. But under the surface of similar practice, there have been shifts in purpose. Her *Essays and Poems*, edited by Robert Halsband and myself in 1977, has had a second, revised edition which is paperback, not hardback.[5] (No hardback was issued.) This means that Oxford were thinking not of libraries but of classrooms. This is a pity, not only because one might wish for simultaneous editions in paper and hardback, for pocket and library, but because the revision is a better text. To say this is not personal vanity; it is a recognition of the way new information undermines old editions. Only two years on from that revision, I already wish I could do more revising. But the inferior text is still, for library users, the one available.

The revisions include valuable new novelties. Several more copies have surfaced of 'Verses on the Death of Mrs. Bowes,' a poem of controlled feminist rage about a fifteen-year-old who died three months after marriage. She was lucky, says Montagu: she'd had the good part, the ecstasy; from then on it would be straight downhill into oppression. Not only do these extra copies underline the poem's popularity, but one of them is demonstrably Montagu's original manuscript.[6] It contains an extra four lines which I had omitted because they are absent from the holograph text which Montagu *kept*.[7] Now I wish I could restore them, because of their presence in this unique original text. Lady Mary dashed it down, with the date, on a

piece of paper; on the other side her friend the feminist Mary Astell
dashed down a companion poem. Each, I believe, shares some flavour
of the other's mind; yet the overall slant is different in each. Astell
agrees with Montagu that marriage was bad news for the bride;
Montagu agrees with Astell that Heaven may offer superior joys. But
Montagu's agreement is inflected with irony. She celebrates the brief
'Rapture' and 'Pleasure' of marriage which Astell sees as tainted: 'Nor
tempted by that Pois'nous Cup to stay / Tasting it scorn'd the draught
and fled away.' She makes no mention of Christ the Bridegroom. Astell
offers a lesson in Christian stoicism, Montagu a wry lament of classic
or libertine flavour.[8]

Here is a parley of minds, a meeting of feminisms: literally two sides
of an act of debate and exchange. By outdating my revised edition, this
manuscript exemplifies the text-as-flux, subject to eternal revision. But
as artefact it exemplifies the poem-as-letter, tied to the moment of its
birth: an original which enjoys an authority which no later revision can
challenge.

Editing Montagu, whether letters or poems or prose pieces, has
always meant building up a volume out of many short and various
copy-texts, most but not all holograph. This is true even in the case of
her previously unpublished *Romance Writings*.[9] The same textual principles, give or take a little elasticity, have served for each genre.
Principles of annotation have been more various, helping to fuel
meditation on the immense range and variety of editors' agendas. For
although innumerable tiny, apparently trivial decisions go to make up
the 'dull duty of an editor' (remember how vigorously Johnson re-
pudiated Pope's 'dull'),[10] there is always an underlying agenda to exert
hidden influence on the tiny details and hence over the shape of the
finished product.

Two separate Montagu editions are recently out: her *Romance Writings* and a new *Selected Letters*.[11] In an ideal editors' world these two
ought to go together with a revised three-volume edition of her letters
for libraries. But Oxford are not willing to do that; nor probably would
any other publisher. The *Romance Writings*, a hardback attractive to
libraries, *ought* to be coupled with a paperback of just one of its several
texts: a marvellous non-novelistic fiction called 'Princess Docile,' which
is a natural text for the classroom. But of course this too is something
no publisher would undertake.

The *Romance Writings* and *Selected Letters* have set two separate kinds
of editorial problem. For the selected letters the issue was how to
render accessible, and how to make exclusions (something I find

difficult). For the *Romance Writings* it was how to mediate between these texts' past oblivion (left in rough draft by their author, ignored by previous scholars), and their potential future as significant – even canonical – texts in the history of English fiction.

Particular editions, we find, have particular purposes and particular audiences. Questions need asking: who is this for? why this now? how does the agenda of this edition compare with others? Behind Montagu's *Complete Letters* lies (as you can tell by the title, not my choice!) a goal of exhaustiveness and closure. The expected audience is posterity, or less grandiloquently the users of reference libraries. Later reflection shows how that edition put their needs first, before the needs of the many private people and common readers who bought and read it for pleasure and historical interest. Such readers deserve a correct, authentic text just as much as library users do. It is safe to bet that few of them took much interest in the full identification of everyone the letters mention. But supplying such identification was and is standard practice in standard editions.

Suppose Lady Mary asks, in a letter, whether Jane Bloggs is married yet. Convention demands that an editor 'identify' Jane Bloggs as 1750–1780, daughter of Tom and Ann (Jones) Bloggs, who married Joe Blow two years later. Ninety-nine readers are not listening. But there may be a hundredth who is working on the Bloggses or the Blows or even the Joneses, and that person is not only listening but making notes. Often such information has no known relevance to Lady Mary; but a scholarly edition has a duty to the scholarly community at large, to the treasure-house or junk-shop of knowledge which we all frequent. And somewhere in those junk-heaps there may even lie an unexpected further link between Lady Mary and Jane Bloggs which will one day make the original information acutely relevant after all. (There is also the matter of the editor's addiction to discovering and purveying such information.)

In matters of annotation, of the adding of information to the text, all judgments ought to be relative, dictated by the occasion. This is easy to say, harder to do. It is desirable for the scholarly community that every literary text of value should be somewhere available, set in a context of all the relevant information about it. That is a kind of mission statement, but it contains a number of slippery terms. How would I define 'text of value'? 'somewhere available'? 'relevant information'? They are all subjective or relative. A text is of value when someone thinks it is; 'somewhere' now includes not only recondite paper sources like PhD theses, but also film and electronic forms; information is relevant, again, when someone thinks it is. If our scholarly community is healthy and vigorous, then probably the very persons whose judgment gives the text its value will be nurturing that judgment on the added information which the text carries in its notes.

Beyond the convention of identifying people, places, and texts lies an almost infinite vista of other things which *might* be annotated. Some readers are bound to find intrusive the explaining which other readers need. The editor's decision where to gloss with meanings will be final but will never be ideal. Some notes make it possible to follow an otherwise baffling issue in the text, while some fill in gaps in life-story which readers need if they want to treat a volume of letters as a kind of biography, but not if they don't. I have a passion for explaining where one place is in relation to another, but some readers will have looked at a map for themselves.

Montagu's writing (not only letters) was inextricably meshed with the actual, partly because that was the style of the time, partly because she wrote for herself or her friends, seldom for a market-wide public. It is instructive to examine some of the processes by which her writings were converted into texts for wider circles of readers, and by which she was converted into an author. Late in life she tended to disclaim this role. She squelched a request for her collected works to adorn a library, protesting, 'upon my word I had never printed a single line in my Life.' (In denying the actual or prospective existence and value of her collected works she rejects the enterprise of Robert Halsband and myself in providing her with a collected works.) She complains about being quoted in other people's books: 'When I print, I submit to be answer'd and criticis'd.'[12] She was not ready to submit to that. The love of fame, she said towards the end of her life, was a juvenile phase, unforgiveable beyond the age of twenty.

Love of fame was a phase she certainly went through. As an adolescent she provided her writings with title-pages or half-titles imitating print. Her first actual publication (an essay in the *Spectator*) presumably resulted from her own agency. Yet it also marked her renunciation of fame. (She was twenty-five.) She refused to let her authorship be known, thus relinquishing any share in the acclaim which fifty years later still clung to anyone who had contributed even a single essay to the *Spectator*.

There is some first-hand evidence, just a little, of her actively arranging her own publication. She dealt directly with James Roberts, who issued her political periodical *The Nonsense of Common-Sense*, 1737–8.[13] She combated his small, unwarrantable liberties with her text – like removing a phrase he thought politically risky, and inserting one which is *risqué* in a different sense, aimed at specifically male readers.[14] So she had living experience of being edited as a woman in a man's world. She said she published the *Nonsense* 'to serve an unhappy worthy Man' (unidentified). This shows her willing *either* to publish – anonymously – in a personal good cause, *or* to use the good cause as excuse to publish.

Another cause was the appearance of her lover Francesco Algarotti's *Newtonianismo per le dame* (1739). She contributed a poem, which appeared with her initials, to the chorus of praise from eminent names which prefaces the volume, published discreetly (from her point of view) abroad.

A crucial proof of willingness to publish would be arranging to publish a major text without the saving excuse of offering anyone personal help. There is such a case, but opinions differ about it: Montagu's treatment of her two manuscript volumes of transcribed and edited letters from Turkey. At some time or times between 1716 and 1724 she devoted careful attention to composing this manuscript. No more than Woolf's *Three Guineas* did it consist of letters actually sent: it was a travel-book in the form of letters. When it was finished, Mary Astell wrote a strong feminist preface to it in prose, as if for a printed book. Astell wanted it published, but she could not persuade the author to do this other than posthumously.

Eventually Montagu committed this text to a clergyman she met in Rotterdam, the Rev. Benjamin Sowden, 'to be dispos'd of as he thinks proper.' This, she said, was her wish, and she signed her statement. She was seventy-two, probably aware that she had breast cancer, nearing the end of a nightmare journey through the war zones between Venice and London. I believe her note on the manuscript volumes constitutes instruction to publish; in a way it fulfils her undertaking to Astell that posthumous publication was acceptable. Mr Sowden's respect for authority, however, led him to contact the head of her family, her son-in-law the Earl of Bute, and then to allow Bute to buy the manuscript for £300.[15] It would never have reached print without the intervention of two travelling Englishmen who borrowed the manuscript overnight from Sowden, but – it turned out – sat up all night transcribing.

One of the copyists, William Beattie, had a friend whose father, Thomas Becket, was a publisher. In 1763 Becket and P.A. De Hondt brought out *Letters Written during her Travels in Europe, Asia, and Africa*, by the Right Honourable Lady M—y W—y M—e. The title-page is really an extended advertisement, but Becket (probably) drafted another: a manuscript 'Advertisement of the Editor'. This gives two reasons for printing: '*First,* Because it was the manifest intention' of the author, and secondly to create for her 'an immortal Monument' and 'shew, as long as the English Language endures, the sprightliness of her wit, the solidity of her judgment, the extent of her knowledge, the elegance of her taste, and the excellence of her *real* character' – which tacitly acknowledges that her character has been unjustly maligned. The Advertisement notes that Montagu allowed copies of the letters to be taken, and feared 'lest her family, thro' an excessive and ill-grounded delicacy, should refuse them to the World.'[16] It thus strategically aligns the audience and publishers with the author herself against *both* her detractors *and* her family. Becket's nerve failed him, however, and this part of the Advertisement was not printed.[17]

This story undermines Montagu's own claim that she did not desire print or fame. Why did she give Sowden the Embassy Letters but not her diary or the fictions now printed in *Romance Writings*? Presumably because only the travel letters were publishable: they were in final form and they were not scandalous. Devious and anonymous publication seems to have been her habit, and her reiterated denial of intent to publish was part of her deviousness. Her transformation into an author, therefore, rested on co-operation from other people. Her action in Rotterdam was consistent with her earlier actions: in youth and age she let her writings circulate privately in a way which was bound to, and which did, end in print.

This seems, flatteringly, to offer the editor an almost partnership relation. But most of those who controlled the passage of her texts into print had motives and goals sharply separate from hers. Edmund Curll, who printed three of her poems as *Court Eclogues* in 1716, aimed to make money and perhaps to embarrass Pope. His action had the effect of embarrassing Montagu with her friends and patrons.[18]

This apparently malicious piracy, early in her career, must have marked Lady Mary's attitude to publication. During her time in Turkey three trusted friends each became a channel, either on purpose or by 'well-intentioned indiscretion,' for an item of her travel writing to get into print.[19] Later, various poems were seized for printing in newspapers or journals, or on their own. Their appearance usually brought some kind of undesirable repercussion to their author. The poem on Mrs Bowes appeared in *The Weekly Journal or Saturday's-Post* and brought a storm of replies, both manuscript and printed. It was attacked not for being disillusioned about marriage, but for being positive about pleasure early on in marriage, which was felt to be disgracefully lewd. Another of Montagu's extemporaneous poems appeared in Aaron Hill's *Plain Dealer*. It came garlanded with praise, but still Lady Mary may not have enjoyed the frame story about a young man in mixed company pulling it out of his pocket to read aloud.

Montagu's very funny, very unsisterly ballad *Virtue in Danger* (1721) appeared as a broadside, going to the tune of 'Chevy Chase,' as 'Written by a Gentleman at St. James's.' The ascription does not destroy the possibility that she wrote it – or even that she printed it. She may secretly have 'placed' some of her hard-hitting polemics which appeared anonymously or pseudonymously, and this may include many pieces never to be identified among the flood of topical poems printed in London throughout the 1720s and 1730s. But the image of her as publishing by stealth has received a blow from James McLaverty's recent, ingenious, and persuasive argument about the printing of *Verses Address'd to the Imitator of Horace*, in which she and Lord Hervey (probably) savaged Pope for his satires. McLaverty argues that Pope himself, wincing over the *Verses'* manuscript circulation at court, had much to gain in the way of sympathy and justification from its public appearance, and is the most likely agent of this outcome. This reading certainly helps to explain Lady Mary's dread of being published, and anger against those who published her.[20]

If she indulged in any secret 'placing,' it ceased when she left England in 1739. Publication by admirers continued: by Horace Walpole in 1747;[21] by Robert Dodsley in his famous *Collection*, 1748;[22] by someone on the staff of the *London Magazine*;[23] by George Colman and Bonnell Thornton in 1755.[24] Malicious publication apparently continued too: Dodsley's sixth edition of 1756 printed a love poem by an older woman to a younger man as having been written by Lady Mary, and the poetic put-down which she says she did write (as if by the man to the woman) as having been written *to* her.[25]

The illicit appearance of her *Letters ... Written during her Travels*, the year after her death, signalled the beginning of her posthumous career as a hot literary property. It was respectfully reviewed,[26] and those reviews show some consciousness of the battle now joined between unlicensed would-be publishers and editors on the one hand, and Lady Mary's descendants on the other. The family became gradually willing to sanction controlled publication in order to fend off less desirable publication. So editing with a view to damaging or to blazoning her reputation was replaced by editing with a view to shoring it up. To her family it was not her literary reputation but her reputation as a woman that mattered.

Lady M-y W-r-t-l-y M-nt-g-e
The Female Traveller
In the Turkish Dress.

Let Men who glory in their better sense,
Read, hear, and learn Humility from hence;
No more let them Superior Wisdom boast,
They can but epual M-nt-g-e at most.

Lady Mary Wortley Montagu as 'The Female Traveller,' from the doubly pirated edition of her *Letters*, 1764 (by kind permission of the Trustees of the British Library).

Looking back at this battle may well make today's editor examine her soul. Which camp do I belong in? Can I claim to share in the morally self-righteous rhetoric of Thomas Becket, granting the author's wishes, building a monument, outwitting slanderers and silencers? I'd *like* to think I did those things. But Becket's Advertisement is clearly, in our terms, a grant-proposal equivalent. His goal is professional gain; his rhetoric is what the project demands. If today's editor is like Becket, she shares his underlying, not his overt, attitudes. She is committed to letting the truth appear even to the author's discredit. She has her own career interests and even financial ends to serve. She resembles not only Becket but more flagrant opportunists – Curll, Richard Phillips – who edited Montagu strictly for what they could get out of her.

On the other hand, what of an editor who emulates the anxious concern for Lady Mary's reputation felt by her family? A modern equivalent might be the hopeless attempt to fashion a politically correct Montagu. There are aspects to her that a late twentieth-century academic feminist might want to play down, as her descendants downplayed her outrageousness.

They had a lot to downplay, because outrageousness had commercial value. After the first *Letters during her Travels* (1763) came a further piracy. It copies the previous text and title-page almost identically, but claims to be 'Printed for A. HOMER in the *Strand*, and P. MILTON in St. *Paul's* Church-yard. MDCCLXIV.' It was apparently published at Edinburgh. Besides the delightful notion of epic poets working as publishers, besides the delightful print of Lady Mary as 'The Female Traveller,' in Turkish dress with feminist inscription, it augments the 1763 text with additional material which is mostly spurious. (A fairly convincing contemporary story has John Cleland – who had once penned a fearsome literary caricature of Lady Mary – writing the spoof parts for a kind of bet.)[27] In 1767 Becket and De Hondt reprinted this as an *Additional Volume* to their edition, and reissued the whole lot together, so that the authentic incorporates and authorizes the spurious. Montagu was, as I said, a hot property.

It is much harder to take evidence out of the record than to put it in. Those misleading editions are still around to be looked at (on the World Wide Web now, as well as in print), and even today scholars working on other subjects not infrequently cite what they take to be an opinion of Lady Mary Wortley Montagu which is actually no such thing.[28]

Montagu's *Poetical Works* joined her Embassy Letters in the public domain in 1768, edited (though without his name) by the young man of letters Isaac Reed.[29] He did a decent job of gathering poems from printed sources, including the outrageous *Verses to the Imitator*. So far, so good. Six years after her death, Montagu had been edited (in a small selection of her total writings) as an eighteenth-century author should be.

A generation later occurred a new find of texts. The publisher Richard Phillips (whose list ran to both pedagogy and scandal)[30] 'purchased of Mr Silverlock, a sollicitor in Serjeant's Inn' either one or two hundred letters, either all or mostly from Lady Mary to her husband, about 'private transactions of her son's.' These clearly had market value. Henry Silverlock found them among Lady Mary's husband's papers and 'purloined' them; Phillips 'determined to publish them.'[31] Here a new issue arose: making the private public, making a book out of originally un-booklike material.

Phillips's stated aim caused panic among Lady Mary's descendants;[32] they set out to prevent it. Phillips did, however, publish letters which were probably at least related to this haul – from Edward Wortley Montagu to Joseph Addison – in *Addisoniana*.[33] He took pains to make Wortley's letters visible in this rag-bag collection. He states his ownership of them in a note early on.[34] He places them eye-catchingly to follow reprints from Lady Mary's spurious letters, gives them a half-title repeating 'never before published,' and labels each one 'Original Letter.'[35] Like Curll, like Becket, he commodifies his author.

Even while printing her husband's letters, Phillips apparently decided that Lady Mary's might bring more in blackmail than in market sales. He 'informd Lord Bute of His intention of giving them to the World,' and Bute, wishing 'to avoid any thing improper appearing,'[36] at once made Phillips an offer, an invitation to publish a larger, authorized edition of Lady Mary, using letters owned by family members, in exchange for allowing Bute to inspect the stolen letters and destroy whatever he thought fit. We have to remember that what is under discussion here is a *first* appearance of *any* actual letters by someone who is now famous above all as a letter-writer. The literary world ought to be grateful to the shady characters Silverlock and Phillips. Without them Montagu's real letters might have been lost like her diary. We might know her *only* as writer of the Embassy Letters and about a third of her extant poems, nothing else.

Bute now proposed respectable, or scholarly, or bowdlerized publication in order to avoid a scandalous one. His plan had the support, more or less, of his next brother, who was heir to Edward Wortley Montagu's fortune.[37] It was not purely a *female* reputation they were seeking to protect; it was family reputation, from the scandal surrounding Edward Wortley Montagu junior.

The deal went through. Phillips got his bigger and better publication (Montagu's *Works* in 5 volumes [1803], which kept selling for years in successive editions); Bute got the chance to suppress some things and sanitize others. Phillips gave up the stolen letters; Bute 'burned the greater part of them.'[38] The man who got the editing job was the Rev. James Dallaway, who was in Bute's debt for church patronage, and had written a book on Constantinople.

Having burned what he judged 'offensive to the Family,' Bute needed to gather material from other relations. One group of letters was felt to be especially scandalous – Lady Mary's cries for help to her sister about Nicholas-François Rémond. This very minor *philosophe* had entrusted her with money to invest in South Sea stock, and when it was of course lost he tried blackmail threats to get her to make it up out of her own pocket. The head of the family wanted these letters burnt; others were less keen. Their owners declined to give the letters up.[39]

Dallaway was an appalling editor. Though he made great play with the authority he drew from using family sources, he actually preferred printed texts to manuscripts whenever he had them. The ones he had were reprints, not originals, and he introduced new, proliferating errors. Where he did use manuscripts, he showed no notion of the integrity of the text, but altered freely, omitting passages without notice and even splicing one letter into another. His underlying agenda was to sanitize. (This means he went well beyond the regular, automatic tidying up which was currently the expected practice dictated by centuries of book-production.) Even the title *Works*, which might sound as if it were claiming higher status than *Letters*, was probably just designed not to sound private.

Dallaway's 'Memoirs' of Lady Mary open with a wrong date and wrong birthplace. (The latter keeps reappearing in modern sources, even though Robert Halsband's life opens quite emphatically on the right one.) About her education Dallaway says virtually the opposite of what she says herself: she criticises her father, and Dallaway's brief is to honour fathers. Though he omits such quantities of Montagu's own writing, he is generous with space to others. He makes a his-and-hers pair of her 'Account of the Court of George I' and her husband's essay on an ostensibly similar topic. He ends his third volume with a letter *from* Wortley about the burgeoning career of their son-in-law Lord Bute. He prints all but one of the known letters which the twentyish Lady Mary sent her friend Anne Wortley (the one he left out is an extended joke about chamber pots), but only eight of the sixty-nine extant ones she sent Edward Wortley before she married him. Letters tending to elopement must have been too controversial.

Dallaway did little annotation. He identified a handful of persons whose status made their genealogies readily accessible, and he was better at getting identifications right than dates of letters. He left most names unidentified, and if Lady Mary was being snide about them he mostly printed a blank.

One can often tell what has caused a particular error: misreading, or misfiling, or ignorance, or tidying, or concealment. Misreading: Lourace for Lovere. Ignorance: Anne Wortley as mother instead of sister to Edward. Tidying: merging unidentified correspondents into identified series, and assigning most letters a place and a year-date even when none appears on the paper and absolutely no evidence for deducing one exists. He assigns 1720s letters variously to Twickenham or Cavendish Square, though Lady Mary did not move to Cavendish Square until 1731. But some of what looks like tidying may be concealment. Lady Mary spent ten years, 1746–56, based at Gottolengo in north Italy, with occasional stays at Lovere. Dallaway gives the place 'Gotolingo' to just one letter (whose subject-matter leaves him no option),[40] and the place 'Louvere' to almost all the others from this time. He presents her as living at Lovere, not Gottolengo, from 1747 to 1756.

He gives a heading of 26 July 1753, 'Louvere, Dairy-house,' to her great garden-description of 1748: five years too late, forty mountainous miles distant. This misled the local scholar G.P. Marinoni, nineteenth-century authority on Lady Mary at Lovere. It is sad to think of Marinoni scouring the valley in search of her dairy-house and coming up with the farm which has been known ever since as Villa Montagu, and of the generations of farming folk offering their gracious hospitality to visiting scholars, all under a complete misapprehension.

Dallaway knew Horace Walpole's allegation that Lady Mary was kept in probably sexual durance at Gottolengo by Ugolino Palazzi. That may have spurred him almost to obliterate Gottolengo from the record. *If* he read her 'Italian Memoir' with attention[41] he may purposely have erased the purchase of the dairy house (which was one of Palazzi's frauds), by placing it beyond Palazzi's sphere of influence.

It is easy today to dismiss Dallaway's excessive respect for patriarchal authority, and to rejoice at the progress made since then by the science of textual editing. But it might be more useful to our own practice to empathize than to condemn. There but for the grace of God goes any of us. Dallaway, faced with literally hundreds of letters, often without date, place, or name of recipient, *had* to impose order. Not only order in theory: the print medium demanded that he decide where each letter should go in sequence, and its demands are just as imperious today. Letters are written in sequence. Editors of letters are historical detectives whose evidence is never likely to be enough. We don't share Dallaway's concern for concealment, but we are not immune from mis-reading, misfiling, ignorance, even tidying. The years are yet to come which will reveal our own mistakes. Thank goodness our own training permits, even encourages, the admission or foregrounding of ignor-ance. This may be the most solid advantage we have.

Dallaway's edition, published by Phillips,[42] omitted much, yet greatly extended Montagu's oeuvre.[43] More finely produced than *Addisoniana*, it boasts an engraved portrait frontispiece and facsimiles. Lady Mary had been published like a noblewoman at last. Reviewers responded appropriately. The conservative, not to say reactionary, *British Critic* tied itself in knots between kowtowing to her 'illustrious descendants' (whom it eulogized lavishly, and took as guarantee of Dallaway's capacity) and doing the same for its patron the public, which, it felt, deserved better than the editorial 'carelessness' which it could not help but notice.[44] Modern parallels spring to mind, where a reviewer perceives something rotten in the work under scrutiny, but is prevented from coming right out and saying so by the status of the editor or somebody else concerned.

Bute was happy to have his ancestress's 'dignified place in the history of polite literature' confirmed by 'the Paris Reviewers.'[45] Dallaway was happy to consider himself a humble friend of the illus-trious family. Phillips was happy to have a popular success: he told Sydney Owenson he wished she could make *The Wild Irish Girl* more like an Irish version of Montagu's Turkish letters.[46] But Phillips was not yet satisfied. Three years later he was hunting, for a new edition, the scandalous Montagu letters which were known to exist, unpub-lished.[47] The family (Bute branch) were not having that. When the next edition appeared – the sixth, reset, 1817 – it was published by a conger of whom Phillips was not one.[48] It included neither the letters about Rémond nor those to Algarotti which Byron wanted to get published.[49]

When he originally selected letters, Bute had consulted brothers and male cousins,[50] but apparently not his youngest sister, Lady Louisa Stuart. She judged Dallaway a 'decided blockhead,' but decided not to intervene after the *Works* appeared. But a generation later, when family interest reawoke, Bute was dead and Lady Louisa alive. A new edition was proposed in 1827. She did most of the work, though two of her nephews were involved. There was a fiction about providing a job for the Rev. Stuart Corbett, who had children and debts;[51] and Lord Wharncliffe, head of the Wortley branch of the family, contributed his noble name and a preface which condescends to Lady Louisa's admirable 'Introductory Anecdotes.' Wharncliffe's agent, John Martin, fielded the financially astute proposals of the new publisher, Richard Bentley.[52]

Lady Louisa, although warmly partisan towards her subject, had a sense of historical integrity. She was willing to print even letters she feared might 'do us no great service.'[53] She expended great efforts in pursuit of extra letters and of information, and used such information as she could get intelligently, even if sometimes wrongly.[54] She improved immeasurably on Dallaway, yet her work is less satisfactory than one might expect from a potentially ideal editor. Wharncliffe got her to agree to pass over 'in silence those mysterious matters which we cannot explain or satisfactorily account for.'[55] 'New' letters were added, some proudly flagged and some, presumably at the owners' wish, unmentioned. Wharncliffe insisted in retaining the spurious letters. He agreed to include those about Rémond, but quarantined them in an appendix.[56]

For noble amateurs, with no editorial principles or knowledge of publishing history, they did pretty well.[57] But basic rethinking was beyond them. They retained the previous edition as base, and made minimal alterations to it (adding only nine letters, for instance, from the courtship) and retaining all those erroneous 'Cavendish Squares' and 'Loveres.'[58] And although he knew Dallaway's Memoir was riddled with error, Wharncliffe retained it along with Lady Louisa's biographical anecdotes, which keep flatly contradicting it. Lady Louisa was thus kept in the ancillary role, commenting, not originating. Being class-bound is the bane of this edition. Unlike the author it serves, it is unable to step beyond its own subculture into literary culture. (It might be worth considering as parallel the need for an academic editor to step beyond her own subculture – it is not only our colleagues who are going to buy our books – into broader literary culture.)

Unhappily one of this edition's reviews – withering, unsigned – was by J.W. Croker, a professional, steeped in knowledge of the period, who had his own immeasurably superior recent edition of Lady Suffolk's correspondence in mind as benchmark, and was famous for his slashing reviews.[59] He had edited Lady Suffolk well; but then he made no claim for her (or she made no claim) as *author*, only as a source for social history. He had quoted Montagu a good deal in his edition (usually unsympathetically) and he knew just how bad Dallaway's was. When Montagu makes a sacrilegious quip and Wharncliffe's edition omits the offensive part,[60] Croker knew, as the family did not, that Walpole had quoted her from manuscript, and been printed, so the cat was already out of the bag.

Croker disliked female claims to authorship.[61] He flatters Lady Louisa oilily, while dismissing her right to judge the acceptability of her grandmother's language or conduct, on the grounds that a respectable unmarried female would *have no idea what was meant by anything said on these topics*.[62] To him Lady Mary's words and conduct were shockingly unacceptable. When Lady Suffolk's correspondent Margaret Bradshaw told sexy stories in a rambling tone and slaphappy syntax, Croker remained calm; when the admired author Montagu told such stories with verbal panache he rebuked her for 'sull[ying] her paper.'

Croker's review used the charge of poor editing as a lever to dislodge Lady Mary from the canonical position which Becket's *Letters* and Dallaway's *Works* had given her. (It is ironical that this charge became crucial just when the editing level had markedly improved.) Each of those earlier collections went through a long, triumphal history of reprints. Wharncliffe's *Letters and Works*, 1837, did not (though it was quickly succeeded, like Dallaway's *Works*, by a second edition correcting some errors). Lady Louisa's complaint that Croker laid 'a prodigious stress upon the most insignificant matters' *could* be read as amateur refusal of the demands of scholarship, but I believe this would be mistaken. (She had just devoted ten years to such insignificant matters herself.) I read it as proto-feminist recognition that Croker had unjustifiably shifted the debate off the literary onto the social, moral, or ideological.[63]

For the rest of the nineteenth century, as reprints of Lady Mary's work (after 1861) succeeded each other and competing versions of her character and literary reputation slugged it out in the press, this was the underlying issue: should she be judged as a professional or an amateur? a writer or a lady? On the whole professional-writer status tended to be denied her, so she was judged by the less friendly standards of ladyhood. Academic activity – *any* academic activity – still relates to this ancient struggle insofar as it confirms her literary status and orientation at the expence of her social one. This is something which is relevant to women writers of far less exalted social status than hers or Lady Louisa's.

Twenty-five years after Wharncliffe's edition, his son and successor gave *carte blanche* to the scholar W. Moy Thomas for a new one.[64]

Thomas worked out a much improved sequence of dates, and removed place-names and other material which is not to be found in the manuscripts. He shifted the letters about Rémond into their proper place in the sequence. But he apparently made no search for extra letters (even those already heard of but not secured, even those actually present in the family archive – like the remainder of the courtship correspondence, which he left with only half a dozen more letters than in Dallaway's edition). He retained the structure of separate correspondences, the memoir by Dallaway, and the spurious letters.

Thomas was a proper scholar, but he did not treat Montagu like a proper author. For that she waited till our own century. Halsband and I have treated her like a proper author – although, as I have said, our work has needed redoing within just a few years, in a way which characterizes women's writings more often than those of men (who have a longer history as objects of scholarship) and private writings more often than those produced for, and quickly transformed into, print. It may seem from what I have said that Montagu has had a lot of editorial attention lately. But that marker of the *truly* canonical author – the simultaneous availability of a scholarly, expensive, 'standard' edition and of cheap paperbacks – seems as far away as ever.

The lesson to be drawn from her story is not, I believe, any easy sense of superiority towards earlier editors. Instead it is a lesson not to take our current academic practices as anything but timebound like everything else. The best prose edition of Montagu before this century was that of Becket and De Hondt, opportunistic commercial publishers with no axe to grind. All the rest had status or ideology invested in her; and as an academic and a feminist, I have both. Today's academic editing practices were shaped by a particular concept of the canon of English Literature, by the needs of a particular education system, and by the goals of a class of intelligentsia which is changing too. I do not want to urge their replacement, and I do not know anything better to replace them with. But let us, meanwhile, treat them as contingent, even precarious.

NOTES

1   David Fairer, 'J.D. Fleeman: A Memoir,' in *Studies in Bibliography* 48 (1995): 1–24, at 11.

2   Fairer, 'Fleeman,' 16, 17, 22.

3   Lady Mary Wortley Montagu, *The Complete Letters of Lady Mary*

Wortley Montagu, ed. Robert Halsband, 3 volumes (Oxford: Clarendon Press, 1965–7).

4 'Verse,' because in those days 'poetry' was a claim I did not feel secure enough to make – although Byron made it, demanding, 'Is not her *Champaigne and Chicken* worth a forest or two? Is it not poetry?' (Lord Byron, *Letters and Journals*, ed. R.E. Prothero, 6 volumes [London: John Murray, 1898–1901], 5: 566).

5 Lady Mary Wortley Montagu, *Essays and Poems and Simplicity, A Comedy*, ed. Robert Halsband and Isobel Grundy (Oxford: Clarendon Press, 1977, 1993).

6 Thistlethwayte MSS, Hampshire Record Office. I am indebted for this discovery to Helen Tasker-Poland.

7 In the *Essays and Poems* Halsband edited the prose and I the poetry.

8 Montagu, *Essays and Poems*, 233; Ruth Perry, *The Celebrated Mary Astell, An Early English Feminist* (Chicago: University of Chicago Press, 1986), 503–4.

9 Lady Mary Wortley Montagu, *Romance Writings*, ed. Isobel Grundy (Oxford: Clarendon Press, 1996).

10 See Samuel Johnson, 'Preface to Shakespeare, 1765,' in *Johnson on Shakespeare*, ed. Arthur Sherbo, The Yale Edition of the Works of Samuel Johnson 7–8, 2 volumes (New Haven: Yale University Press, 1968), 1: 94.

11 Lady Mary Wortley Montagu, *Selected Letters*, ed. Isobel Grundy (Harmondsworth: Penguin, 1997).

12 Montagu, *Complete Letters*, 3: 38–9, 95.

13 'To be continued as long as the Author thinks fit, and the Publick likes it' (Montagu, *Essays and Poems*, 105–49, at 105).

14 She likened good advice to medicine which has to be forced on a reluctant child for its own good; he added a comparison with a 'tender lover' forcing sex on a woman (Montagu, *Essays and Poems*, 112).

15 Hannah Sowden, the minister's daughter, tried to explain in 1804 why this should not be regarded in the light of taking a bribe (Bath, 31 January 1804: *Edinburgh Review* 4 [1805]: 254–6).

16 Some other copy may have been the Montagu letters once 'consigned to the care' of the obscure Miss Wilkinsons, then in Paris, who had some purchase on literary life in their friendship with Johnson's friend Anna Williams. The last of them, Jane, died during the 1770s (Phillipina Knight in *Johnsonian Miscellanies*, ed. George Birkbeck Hill [Oxford: Clarendon Press, 1897], 2: 171–2, 174–5).

17 Beattie MSS, Central Public Library, Finchley Road, London.

18 As Robert Halsband points out, Pope's revenge was probably aimed at protecting Gay rather than Montagu (*Life of Lady Mary Wortley Montagu* [Oxford: Clarendon Press, 1956], 54).

19 Two letters in French, printed through Antonio Conti and an unknown female friend; 'Constantinople. To [her uncle William Feilding],' who eased it into print (Montagu, *Complete Letters*, 1: 374–8, 403–4; Montagu, *Essays and Poems*, 206–10).

20 James McLaverty, ' "Of which being publick the Publick judge": Pope and the Publication of *Verses Address'd to the Imitator of Horace*,' *Studies in Bibliography*, forthcoming.

21 He printed her *Six Town Eclogues, with Other Poems*, at Strawberry Hill in 1747. This may have been a dubious favour. Ann Cline Kelly notes that while posthumous works encoded 'the idea of transcendence over time and mortality,' collections by a single living author were read as 'manifestations of vanity' or 'egotism' ('The Semiotics of Swift's 1711 *Miscellanies*,' *Swift Studies* 6 [1991]: 59–68, at 62).

22 He included her in his best-selling anthology *Collection of Poems* (1748), and promoted her to volume one in his second, much better produced, edition the same year. Michael F. Suarez points out Horace Walpole's probable agency in the *Collection*, its close links with Pope, and the legitimating effect of the second edition's aesthetic quality ('Trafficking in the Muse: The Sale and Distribution of Dodsley's *Collection of Poems*, 1748–1782,' *Studies on Voltaire and the Eighteenth Century* 304 [1992]: 1098–101). Elizabeth Carter was the only other woman in the original three volumes. Dodsley sought permission to label Lady Luxborough's work in volume 4, 'by a Lady' (29 October [1754], *The Correspondence of Robert Dodsley*, ed. James E. Tierney [Cambridge: Cambridge University Press, 1988], 182).

23 Its editor was Isaac Kimber: see *A Ledger of Charles Ackers: Printer of The London Magazine*, ed. D.F. McKenzie and J.C. Ross (Oxford: Oxford University Press, 1968), 7.

24 *Poems by Eminent Ladies* (London: R. Baldwin, 1755), 157–84. Chantel Lavoie draws my attention to the fact that Montagu is the only author in this volume to be given no biographical note – probably because of her rank.

25 Montagu, *Essays and Poems*, 263–4.

26 Of reviews in 1763, the *Monthly* 28 (1763): 84–94, 461–73 and 29 (1763): 57–65, gave the letters one notice per volume, endorsed their authenticity, and closed with an apostrophe to 'most elegant, spirited, amiable Lady Mary!' which could not possibly have been addressed to a male writer. The *Annual Register* 6 (1763): 290–307, made them

one of its half-dozen annual choices. It praised lavishly, but seemed obsessed with the question of authenticity – which it doubted, perhaps in deference to Montagu's family. The *Critical* (1763): 426-35, said it would quote rather than praise, but claimed, in opening, that women write better letters than men and, in closing, that the volumes were being read by 'all the polite world.'

27 John Cleland, *Memoirs of a Coxcomb* (London: R. Griffiths, 1751). One of the additional 'Embassy' letters refers to Percy Lodge on the Thames, a house which was not given that name till the 1740s. The Homer-Milton edition *without* the spurious extras was re-pirated as one volume in 1766, at South Berwick (says the Bodleian catalogue), with the most playfully inventive use of printer's flowers to divide letter from letter that I have ever seen.

28 The additional letters were given a mistaken boost when Lady Mary's daughter 'looked into' the 1767 volume (she knew nothing of the epic poets' piracy of a piracy) and pronounced it genuine. Since it does contain genuine material a quick look might be easily satisfied.

29 He wrote the first account of the Johnson-Chesterfield quarrel (*Westminster Magazine*, 1774) and perhaps an account of Johnson in the *European Magazine*, January 1785 (*The Early Biographies of Samuel Johnson*, ed. O M Brack, Jr., and Robert E. Kelley [Iowa City: University of Iowa Press, 1974], 46), and collected scurrilous news items about Laetitia Pilkington (his copy of her *Memoirs*, Bodleian 8vo Z 150 Art. B.S.). His Montagu edition was reprinted in 1781 (Tonson, Hodges, et al.) and 1784 (Osborne and Griffin).

30 He published Anna Letitia Barbauld's edition of Richardson's *Correspondence* as well as obvious money-spinners and many pedagogical texts.

31 James Dallaway (employed as Bute's editor, and so an authoritative source) in his set of Montagu's *Works* (1803), now owned by Mr Buist-Wells of London, UK; Bute to the Earl of Fife, 11 June 1804, MS in copy of Montagu, *Works* (1803), sold at Hodgsons, 21 April 1949; to his cousin John Francis Erskine of Mar, 8 April 1803, Mar and Kellie MSS, Scottish Record Office, GD 124/15/1716; Joseph Farington, *The Diary of Joseph Farington April 1803–December 1804*, ed. Kenneth Garlick and Angus Macintyre, 6 volumes (New Haven: Yale University Press, 1979), 6: 2133.

32 Among, that is, her senior grandson (now first Marquess of Bute), his banker Thomas Coutts, and his cousin John Francis Erskine of Mar (1741–1825). Erskine was elder grandson of Lady Mary's sister Lady Mar, son and heir of Lady Frances Erskine and James Erskine of

Grange, restored to the Earldom of Mar in 1824 (Mar MSS GD 124/15/1716/1–5).

33 *Addisoniana*, ed. Sir Richard Phillips, 2 volumes (London: T. Davison, 1803).

34 *Addisoniana*, 1: v.

35 *Addisoniana*, 1: 236. Wortley's letters include boasting of how easy and pleasant he finds it to live on 'a very small income' – something about him which, owing to Pope, might still resonate somewhere in the public's memory. They make various plans for sharing lodgings with Addison – which would be most interesting to readers (as yet non-existent) of Lady Mary's courtship letters.

36 Mar MSS, GD 124/15/1716/1.

37 James Archibald Stuart, later James Archibald Stuart Wortley Mackenzie (1747–1818).

38 Dallaway's annotation in the Buist-Wells set. The one surviving letter which is identified as having passed through Silverlock's hands (now bound in this set) does nothing to explain Bute's concern (Montagu, *Selected Letters*, 512).

39 'As the remaining entertaining Letters of Ldy Mary tho' many of Them are improper for the Public Eye, are still too precious to be destroyed, I hope that your Lordship will not be displeased at my keeping of Them' (Erskine of Mar in Mar MSS GD 124/15/1716/3–4).

40 24 April 1749, Montagu, *Complete Letters*, 2: 424–6.

41 Printed in Montagu, *Romance Writings*, 81–105.

42 *The Works of the Right Honourable Lady Mary Wortley Montagu. Including her Correspondence, Poems and Essays, Published By Permission From Her Genuine Papers*, 5 volumes (London: Richard Phillips, 1803). A 'fifth edition' (1805) added the letters to Frances Hewet, the first MSS from beyond the immediate family.

43 It adds many unprinted poems and five essays, four from MS. It includes, as twentieth-century editions do not, Lady Mary's translation of Epictetus (written at 21), a sample of her hand, and others of Pope, Addison, Young, Fielding, and Sarah Duchess of Marlborough.

44 Article 9, *The British Critic* 22 (1803): 643–8. It also, however, opened the debate about Lady Mary's character and motives which nineteenth-century editions of her writings were to keep so long alive. Ill-health, it says, was 'the cause or pretext' of her going abroad in 1739.

45 Letter to Lord Fife, quoted above. He probably did not know that her most enthusiastic French reviewer to date was still Voltaire.

46 Sydney Owenson, Lady Morgan, *Lady Morgan's Memoirs*, 2 volumes (London: W.H. Allen, 1862), 1: 254.

47 A Mrs Anna Munro had contacted him positively confirming their existence, which had been denied (5 September 1806, Mar MSS, GD 124/15/1716/6).

48 Longman, Hurst, Rees, Orme, and Brown; John Murray; and Baldwin, Cradock, and Joy.

49 Some were in the hands of John Murray, Byron's publisher and one of the conger.

50 Inscription in set of Montagu, *Works* (1803) in the Deering Library, Northwestern University.

51 Wharncliffe MSS, Sheffield City Archives, 420, 439/1a. He got so far as drafting an undated 'Preface of the Editor' which thanks owners for lending the letters whose loan Lady Louisa had negotiated (23 April 1827, Wharncliffe 439/17, 439/28–9, 439/39).

52 He averred that 'the publication would be a matter of honor ... rather than of profit,' but also stressed the expense of notes and prints, quoting comparative figures on Lord Dover's correspondence and Walpole's unpublished letters to Mann (Wharncliffe MSS 439/45; Michael L. Turner, *Index and Guide to the Lists of the Publications of Richard Bentley & Son 1829–1898* [Bishops Stortford: Chadwyck-Healey, 1975], 150).

53 These were the letters to Philippa Mundy (C.B. Massingberd, December 1833, Wharncliffe MSS 439/41). Lady Louisa regretted the lost, 'very clever and rather *paw*' letters to Lady Buck (30 December 1833, to 1st Baron Wharncliffe, Wharncliffe MS 439/42); Francis Mundy, January 1836, Wharncliffe 439/49). Sir Henry Campbell checked out the market value of his letters before offering them, but found it disappointing (30 December 1833, 1 April 1734, Wharncliffe 439/40, 439/43).

54 For instance, 'Lady Lechmere's catastrophe' was quite naturally interpreted as meaning her death, and a single letter to Lady Mar was therefore dated a decade after the rest of the correspondence. Lady Lechmere, though, had only attempted suicide.

55 16 December 1836, Wharncliffe MSS 439/54.

56 Lady Louisa to Lord Wharncliffe, 8 March [1837], Wharncliffe MSS 439/56; Wharncliffe to Bentley, 9 October 1836, Bentley Papers, University of Illinois. Lady Louisa later called this appearance 'awkward,' but it is not clear if she meant the quarantining or the story itself.

57 Though Dallaway had related the story of the *Additional Volume*, Wharncliffe thought the spurious letters first appeared in a 1789 reprint, no doubt because this was the edition to hand.

58 Copy-text was clearly a marked set of an earlier edition. Wharncliffe's preface says what they meant to do, not what they did. Verifying and

revising dates of letters was done for those to Lady Mar (where it was *obvious* that a problem existed), but not for those written abroad.

59 *The Quarterly Review* 58 (1837): 147–96.

60 'Father Adam shines through his whole progeny; he first eat the apple like a sot and then turn'd Informer like a Scoundrel' (Montagu, *Complete Letters*, 2: 83).

61 His venom at A.L. Barbauld's most public poem clearly stems not from her views but from her assumption of masculine-type authority (Margaret Favretti, 'Anna Barbauld's "Eighteen Hundred and Eleven"' [Paper delivered at the conference 'Rethinking Women's Poetry 1730–1930,' Birkbeck College, London, 21 July 1995]).

62 Nothing could have been more annoying for Lady Louisa, whose young days had passed before women were expected to be *quite* that ignorant of life.

63 She detested Croker's 'impertinence & flippancy': 'He has read the book merely to find out what he could cavil at' (to Lord Wharncliffe, 8 March [1837], Wharncliffe MSS 439/56).

64 Called the third, in a gesture towards the authority of the earlier Wharncliffe edition.

4 Editorial Conundra in the Texts of Katherine Philips

When I acquired the rights to Patrick Thomas's edition of the poems and letters of Katherine Philips in 1988, my intention was simply to publish it as the most authoritative account of the poet's work then in existence.[1] Because I knew that, as the vicar of a cluster of Welsh hill-parishes and the conscientious father of a very young family, Dr Thomas was too busy to be personally involved, I undertook to prepare his PhD thesis for publication, and succeeded in incorporating a distressing number of my own errors in the process. It would not at that time have occurred to me to take the liberty of systematically reviewing Thomas's work or questioning his methods. The work of Peter Beal and Elizabeth Hageman, among others, has since demonstrated that there was one important manuscript source, a series of contemporary copies (some autograph), and various contemporary printings of which Thomas had no knowledge.[2] These deficiencies in our edition are less material than my growing conviction that all is less well in the Orinda canon than is generally realized.

The most basic editorial principles obliged Thomas to accept as copy-texts all of Katherine Philips's autograph copies, even though the most important of these, National Library of Wales MS 775B, dubbed by Beal the Tutin MS, must have been made before the Restoration.[3] The possibility that Orinda herself continued to work on her poems and that variant versions of these early poems are the result of later authorial emendation should not be ignored. More problematic is Thomas's acceptance of the copy of seventy-six poems made by Sir Edward Dering as more authoritative than alternative sources for poems not to be found in Philips's autograph.[4] Thomas assumed that Dering's copies would have been made from Orinda's autograph when he and the poet were both in Dublin in 1662–3. However, examination of the manuscript shows that it is written on paper from the same batch as Dering's letter-book in the University of Cincinnati Library, which was copied from scattered papers many years after the letters were originally written.[5] Further examination is needed to establish when the copy of the poems was made and whether it is in fact directly descended from Orinda's autograph.

Thomas believed that Dering was a reliable copyist. The truth seems to be that Dering had scant regard for accuracy or authenticity in general, and did not scruple to improve Orinda's work as he copied it. Comparison of the Dering MS with the Tutin MS shows Dering habitually altering locutions such as 'does' to 'doth,' 'has' to 'hath,' 'your' to 'thy,' and singular abstract nouns to the plural. Such changes are a worse distortion than accidental corruptions, because they exert a pervasive effect on Orinda's tone, muting her characteristic direct-ness. Some substitutions, such as, 'heaven-like' for 'god-like' in 'To the truly noble Sir Ed: Dering (the worthy Silvander) on his dream, and navy,'[6] 'while' for 'since' in 'Friendship's Mysterys,'[7] seem deliberate; others, such as 'red-rose' for 'red-crosse' in 'Content, to my dearest Lucasia,'[8] seem pure carelessness.

Conversely, Thomas had little time for the copyist of National Library of Wales MS 776B, which Beal calls the Rosania MS, the fullest transcription of Orinda's work, which was made soon after the poet's death for presentation to Mary Montagu, her Rosania, who nursed her in her last illness.[9] Thomas judged the hand to be professional; Beal correctly identifies it as 'a single, neat but somewhat varying, non-professional hand.'[10] Thomas rejected the Rosania MS as a copy-text because in many of the poems lines are missing. These have not been dropped by chance or negligence; in every case whole couplets and whole syntactic units have been removed. The poems have been deli-berately shortened and, in many cases, the excision is an improvement. The first of these can be seen in the second poem in the collection, 'A Sea Voyage from Tenby to Bristol':

> One of the rest, pretending to more wit,
> Some small Italian spoke, but murther'd it;
> For I (thankes to Saburra's letters) knew
> How to distinguish 'twixt the false and true;
> But to oppose them there as mad would be
> As contradicting a presbyterie.
> Let it be Dutch, quoth I, e'en what you please;

For him that spoke it might be bread and cheese.
So softly moves our Barke, which none controules,
As are the meetings of agreeing soules.

In the Rosania manuscript the two couplets beginning 'But to oppose them ...' have been suppressed.[11] Similarly, two couplets are deleted from the third poem in the manuscript, a quatrain from the fourth, eleven couplets from the sixth, two couplets from the eighth and from the eleventh, seven quatrains from the twelfth, three couplets from the fourteenth, one couplet from the fifteenth, five couplets from the six-teenth reducing it by a third, four quatrains from the eighteenth, four couplets from the nineteenth, and so on. Of a total of ninety-one poems, twenty appear to have been pruned in this fashion. If the person who pruned them was the poet, we do violence both to her art and to her reputation by insisting on printing the longer versions found in earlier sources.

If we examine the other texts in the Rosania MS we find among them an exact transcription of the 1663 printing of *Pompey: A Tragoedy* together with a transcription of the rough first draft of Orinda's unfinished line by line translation of Corneille's *Horace*, which can be seen to be a faithful and complete rendering of the French original.[12] These texts indicate that the copyist of the Rosania MS was neither an innovator nor an improver. It would follow that the emendations to the poems in the compilation were already to be found in the copy-text. To decide on the available evidence to print the shortened versions would have been an unacceptably radical decision for Orinda's first modern editor to make, but the problem remains.

The question of whether Orinda herself is responsible for changes in her texts is more than usually vexed. Like all other women writers of the period, she solicited corrections of her work from better-educated people, that is, from gentlemen. Though she sometimes asked for corrections to be sent to her so that she might incorporate them in her own copies, she was also content to have her work sent forward with corrections that she had never seen. On 3 May 1662 she sent her poem 'To her royall highnesse the Dutchesse of Yorke, on her command to send her some things I had wrote' to Cottrell with the stipulation

that it shall not be seen at Court, till you have first put it in a better Dress, which I know you will do, if it be capable of Improvement; if it be not, commit [it] to the Flames.[13]

When Cottrell passed on another poem, 'To the Queens Majesty, on her late Sickness and Recovery,' without altering it in any way, Orinda announced her intention of quarrelling heartily with him.[14] Strangely, none of the presentation copies of poems addressed by Orinda to members of the royal family has survived, so we have no way of knowing how the surviving texts compare with what those exalted personages actually saw.

The authoritative version of *Pompey: A Tragoedy*, Orinda's translation of Corneille's *La Mort de Pompée*, is necessarily taken to be the 1663 Dublin printing, published immediately after the play's staging under the auspices of the Earl of Orrery at the Smock Alley Theatre.[15] As Orinda wrote her translation at Orrery's request and was present at the performance, it seems inevitable that she would have seen her work through the press. The fact that the published text differs markedly from the only surviving contemporary manuscript, National Library of Wales MS 21867B, would seem to require an explanation. A letter of Orinda to Poliarchus, undated but certainly of November 1662, reveals that:

> There are, tho' much against my Will, more Copies of it abroad than I could have imagin'd; but the Dutchess of Ormond would not be refus'd one, and she and Philaster have permitted several persons to take Copies from theirs. However, I disclaim them all till I see the Corrections you have made, which I beg of you to send me by the first Opportunity, that I may, before I go hence, correct the other Copies by yours.[16]

The manuscript is written in a small, neat, non-professional hand, with few elisions and corrections, as if for presentation. The songs, which were written last in order to provide an excuse for music and dancing between the acts, are added in another hand at the end of the manuscript. Katherine Philips's hand can be identified in some of the occasional emendations and at the end of the song that closes Act 3, where she has added the stage business and an extra speech, which has no equivalent in Corneille:

> Then follows a military Dance, as part of Cornelia's Dream after
> which she starts up in amazement, & say's
>   What have I seen? and whether is it gone
>   How great the vision! and how quickly done!
>   Yet if in Dreams we future things can see,
>   There's still some Joy, laid up in Fate for me.[17]

Thy fate shall waft thee … one ashore
And to thy Pompey thee Restore

Where First she Leave of sad remorse
Weell entertaine our Spotless Vowes
In Beauteous and Immortall groues

There none a guilty Crown shall weare
Nor Cæsar be Dictator there
Nor shall Cornelia shed a teare

*Then follow's a military Dance, as part of Cornelia's Dream
after which she starts up in amazement, & say's*

*What have I seen? & whither is it gone?
How great ye vision? & how quickly done?
Yet if in dreams, we future things can see
There's still some Joy, layd up in Fate for me.*

And then goes out.

At the conclusion of the song written for the end of Act III of *Pompey: A Tragoedy*, the stage business and the interpolated speech by Cornelia are added in Katherine Philips's hand. National Library of Wales MS 21867B, f. 38 (by kind permission of the National Libary of Wales).

What this proves is that Orinda had the manuscript in her hands very shortly before the performance, for the songs and business were decided upon in the course of production. It is even possible that the manuscript represents the script as it was performed. In the printed version more than 120 lines have been substantially rewritten.

References in Orinda's letters to difficulties in her text show that she is unlikely to have done the rewriting herself. After he saw the translation in December 1662, Cottrell appears to have written to Orinda regarding the use of certain words as bi-syllables, for she replied on 10 January 1663:

> As for the words *Heaven and Power*, I am of your Opinion too, especially as to the latter; for the other may, I think be sometimes so plac'd, as not to offend the Ear, when it is used in two Syllables.[18]

However, by April 1663 when the printed copy was in circulation, Orinda was embarrassed to discover that examples of her bi-syllabic pronunciation of both words were still to be found in it. She wrote to Cottrell:

> By my Lady Tyrrel, who took shipping last Friday for Chester, I have sent you a packet of printed Pompey's to dispose of as you think fit ... but before you part with any, pray mend these two Lines, Act 5. Scene 2.
> If Heaven, which does persecute me still,
> Had made my Power equal to my Will.[19]
> My objection to them is, that the words *Heaven and Power* are us'd as two Syllables each; but to find fault with them is much easier to me, than to correct them.[20]

In the manuscript, the copyist had turned some of the unfortunate bi-syllables into monosyllables by eliding the offending 'e's so that the lines did not scan, only to have them restored in Orinda's hand. In the printed version some of these problem lines have been rewritten. Where the manuscript has

> And hee who then would equity obey
> Must not his reason but his power weigh

in which 'power' is pronounced as two syllables, the printed version substitutes:

> And he who then Affairs would rightly weigh
> Must not his Reasons, but his power obey.[21]

Another line in the manuscript

> Since too much Power will theire strength Orewhelm

was altered to:

> Those too much Power would quickly overwhelm.[22]

Examples of 'heaven' scanned as a bi-syllable are also corrected:

> When shee her Pompeys Murther did Perceive,
> Her wofull hands to heaven shee did heave.

became:

> By dreadful shrieks, she try'd his Life to shield,
> Then hopeless up to Heav'n her hands she held.[23]

Grammar too presented Orinda with problems. In June 1663 she wrote to Cottrell:

> Sir Edward Dering has desir'd me to ask your Opinion concerning
> these two Lines in the last Scene of the Play
>   I know I gain another Diadem,
>   For which none can be blam'd but Heav'n and him.
> His objection is, that *him* is scarce Grammar; he says it should be *he*: I
> am not Critick enough to resolve this Doubt, and therefore leave it
> wholly to your Determination.[24]

Other examples of this kind of grammatical blunder had been corrected in the printed version. Act 4, scene 4, lines 21–2 in the manuscript read:

> No Pompeys blood forever must deny
> All Correspondence between thee and I.

In print, this was changed to:

> No, *Pompey's* blood must all commerce deny,
> Betwixt his Widow and his Enemy.[25]

Another class of emendations derives from an attempt to update *Pompey* by incorporating Corneille's revisions for the collected edition of 1660, Orinda having availed herself of an earlier edition.[26] All these revisions may have had Orinda's sanction, but the question remains whether we should think of *Pompey* as the product of a collaboration rather than all Orinda's own work.

It is a truism of women's literary history that the 1664 edition of *Poems by the Incomparable Mrs K. P.* was unauthorised. Texts derived from this source are regarded with suspicion, readings from the 1667 *Poems by the most deservedly admired Mrs Katherine Philips the Matchless Orinda* being preferred. Close examination of the sequence of events suggests that the truth is clean contrary, that *Poems* 1664 was not unauthorised and that variant readings from *Poems* 1667 are unacceptable.

Katherine Philips had appeared in print at least four times by the time *Poems* 1664 was announced. 'To the Memory of the most Ingenious and Virtuous Gentleman Mr. William Cartwright, my much valued Friend' appears as the first of the fifty-four commendatory poems in *Comedies, Tragicomedies, with other Poems by Mr. William Cartwright*, published by Humphrey Moseley in 1651. Philips's poem, signed K.P., is chivalrously placed before the rest, which are all by men who are presented in descending order of rank beginning with the Earl of Monmouth. The published version differs in important respects from Orinda's autograph, most significantly in the line:

> Rescue us from our dull imprisonment,

which as printed read:

> Shall rescue us from this imprisonment.[27]

We might wonder why, if she sanctioned the revision, Orinda did not incorporate it in her own copy.

In 1655, four years after the Cartwright poem, two more of Philips's poems appeared in Henry Lawes's *Second Book of Airs and Dialogues*. Though others of the contributors appeared merely as initials, Katherine Philips's poem 'To the much honoured Mr Henry Lawes on his Excellent Compositions in Music'[28] was signed with her full name, which also appeared on the setting of a poem of hers entitled 'Mutuall Affection betweene *Orinda* and *Lucatia*,' more usually known as 'Friendship's Mysterys.'[29] The text of the former as printed departs from Orinda's autograph in nine instances, one of which ('Scarrs' for 'stars') is an obvious corruption, while five of the other variant readings can be found in no other source. The text of the second disagrees with the autograph in three cases, one of which, 'Graces' for 'Grows,' is an obvious corruption. In this collection Orinda was surrounded by her coterie; three poems by Silvander, otherwise known as Sir Edward Dering, appear in settings by his wife, Orinda's friend Mary Harvey, together with a poem addressed by Cratander, Sir John Berkenhead, to Lucasia, Philips's closest friend, Anne Owen, and a song by Philaster, John Jeffreys. It would seem from this that at least during the Interregnum neither Orinda nor her circle had serious objections to appearing in print, even in rather garbled versions.

Though *Pompey* was published anonymously, Philips's authorship was well-known. The same Dublin bookseller and printer included her work in a miscellany, *Poems by Several Persons*, published at almost the same time. She wrote to Poliarchus on 15 May 1663:

> I intend to send you by the first Opportunity a Miscellaneous Collection of Poems, printed here; among which, to fill up the Number of his Sheets, and as a Foil to the others, the Printer has thought fit, tho' without my Consent or Privity, to publish two or three Poems of mine, that had been stolen from me; but the others are worth your reading.[30]

Though Philips is careful to deny complicity, there is no hint here of outrage. We may suspect that, despite her disclaimers, she should have been delighted to find her work not only included in a volume with Orrery's and Cowley's, but celebrated by both of them. Orrery's 'To Orinda' is the second poem in the miscellany,[31] Cowley's 'Ode. On Orinda's Poems,' the fourteenth,[32] followed by 'Ode. On Retirement. By a Lady.'[33] The collection also includes 'To the Right Honourable, the Lady Mary Butler, at her Marriage to the Lord Cavendish'[34] and 'The Irish Greyhound,'[35] both 'By a Lady,' that is, Katherine Philips. For the Stump Cross Books edition Thomas, who did not know of the survival of a single exemplum of this edition, used Dering's text. In Dering's version, the third line of the retirement ode reads:

> And me too long thy football made

whereas the Dublin editor has supplied:

> And me too long thy restless ball hast made.

This version appears in no other source, and must be considered the Dublin editor's emendation, as must other substitutions, e.g., 'wilt' for 'dost,' 'mortals' for 'worldlings,' 'And where bright angels gladly would resort' for 'Where angels would officiously resort,' and 'subjects' for 'subdues.' The wedding poem for the Lady Mary Butler exhibits one variant to be found in no other version, 'always' for 'still do,' a change prompted by political tact. The text of 'The Irish Greyhound' has also been tinkered with: 'By which' becomes 'From whence,' 'And' 'But,' 'does make' 'hath made,' and 'Man's Guard would now be, not his sport' becomes 'He would Man's Guard be, not his sport.' Once again, if Dering is to be trusted, Katherine Philips seems neither to have accepted nor rejected these alternative versions which, from the point of view of smoothness, appear to be improvements.

Whoever supplied the Dublin printer with his copies it was not Cowley, eleven of whose poems make up the bulk of the book, together with two by Sir Peter Pett, one by Clement Paman, and Orinda's three. When Herringman published Cowley's *Verses Written upon Several Occasions* later in the same year, he was obliged to announce:

> Most of the verses, which the author had no intention to publish,
> having been lately printed at Dublin without his consent or knowl-
> edge, and with many, and some gross mistakes in the impression, he
> hath thought fit for his justification in some part to allow me to
> reprint them here.[36]

By this time Orinda had spent the better part of three years building a literary career for herself; the announcement of a forthcoming book of poems in *The Newes* of 14 January 1663/4 was the logical next step. The publisher Richard Marriott, son of the distinguished literary publisher John Marriott, had inherited an impressive list of literary copyrights to which since the beginning of the 1640s he added more of his own, including works by Donne, Quarles, Wotton, and Richard Brome. He published the first and twelve of the succeeding editions of Izaak Walton and the first authorised edition of *Hudibras*. Some of his activities in the 1660s, by which time he was one of the distinguished senior members of his profession, suggest a direct link with Orinda. In 1660 and 1661 he published editions of compilations by John Ogilby, who directed the production of Philips's *Pompey* in Dublin, and at the beginning of 1663 he published *The Assembly-Man* by Sir John Berkenhead, Orinda's Cratander. If his edition of Orinda's *Poems* was in fact unauthorized, it is the only instance of Marriott's being connected with a pirated work. Only days before the Orinda débâcle, he had taken space in *Mercurius Publicus* to warn the public against 'a most false imperfect copy' of *Hudibras*, to the authentic version of which he had exclusive copyright. Four days after he advertised Orinda's book he announced its withdrawal:

> Publication being made upon last Thursday of the Poems of Madam Catherine Phillips newly printed for Richard Marriott, it is now the wish and desire of the said Richard Marriott to notify that whereas he was fully persuaded both of the correctness of the copy, and of that ingenious lady's allowance to have them printed, that now he finds neither the one nor the other, according to his expectation: which is a double injury, and that he intends to forbear the sale of them, being not without hope, that this false copy may produce the true one.[37]

As seventeenth-century editions go, *Poems* 1664 is unusually good. Every one of the poems is an authentic work by Orinda. Though Orinda may have been told that the poems were abominably transcribed, and may have believed it, in fact they were not. The proportion of corruptions and emendations is actually smaller than we have seen Philips tolerate in other printings. It was not until Friday, 29 January that Orinda wrote to Cottrell:

> I am so oblig'd to you for the generous and friendly Concern you take in the unfortunate Accident of the unworthy publishing of my foolish Rhymes, that I know not which way to express, much less to deserve, the least part of so noble an Obligation. Philaster gave me a hint of this Misfortune last Post, and I immediately took an Opportunity of expressing to him the great but just Affliction it was to me, and beg'd him to join with you in doing what I see your Friendship had urged you both to do without that Request.[38]

In other words, the withdrawal of *Poems* 1664 was forced without consulting the author, before the author could be consulted. It is only fair to point out that the dating of the 29 January letter could be disputed; Orinda's letters to Poliarchus were not printed until 1704, and then in completely rewritten versions.[39] Of more authority is a surviving autograph letter to Dorothy Temple, clearly dated 22 January, in which Philips claimed to have instructed Jeffreys herself:

> some most dishonest person hath got some collection of my Rimes as I heare, and hath deliverd them to a printer who I understand is Just upon putting them out, and this hath so extreamly disturb'd me, both to have my private follys so unhandsomly exposd, and the beleif that I beleive the most part of the world are apt enough to have, that I conniv'd at this ugly accident, that I have been on a Rack ever since I heard it and though I have written to Colonel Jeffreys, (who first sent me word of it) to get the Printer punish'd the book call'd in, and me some way publickly vindicated, yet I shall need all my friends to be my Champions to the Critticall and malicious, that I am so Innocent of this pittifull design of a Knave to get a Groat, that I was never more vex'd at anything, and that I utterly disclaim whatever he hath so unhandsomely expos'd.[40]

The printer was never punished and the copies were never destroyed. No action was taken by the Stationers' Company of which Marriott was a leading member and from which he had duly secured licence to publish.[41] The letters to Dorothy Temple and to Cottrell are hardly reconcilable and do little to dispel doubts as to Orinda's candour. Orinda also put a good deal of effort into penning a public disclaimer which was enclosed with her letter to Cottrell for circulation as he thought fit:

> Your last generous concern for me, in vindicating me from the unworthy usage I have received at London from the Press, doth as much transcend all your former favours, as the injury done me by that Publisher and Printer exceeds all the troubles that I remember I ever had. All I can say to you for it, is, that though you assert an unhappy, it is yet a very innocent person, and that it is impossible for malice itself to have printed those Rimes (you tell me are gotten abroad so impudently) with so much abuse to the things, as the very publication of them at all, though they had been never so correct, had been to me, to me (Sir) who never writ any line in my life with an intention to have it printed, and who am of Lord Falkland's mind, that said,

He danger fear'd than censure less,
Nor could he dread a breach like to a Press.

And who (I think you know) am sufficently distrustful of all, that my
own want of company and better employment, or others' commands
have seduc'd me to write, to endeavor rather that they should never
be seen at all, than that they should be expos'd to the world with
such effrontery as now they most unhappily are.[42]

The poor woman was obliged not only to countenance the suppression
of her work but to disclaim all literary ambition, in plain contradiction
of the facts of her career up to that point. She had happily sent to
Cottrell copies of the Dublin printing of *Pompey* for distribution
amongst interested parties and sent him *Poems by Several Persons* as
well. Hardly a post went without her including some example of her
work for him to circulate. Cottrell must have known that her pleadings
in these letters were disingenuous, but he was unrelenting. If she was
to have the reputation of a gentlewoman, she could not afford to be
seen to exhibit her talents and feelings to the multitude. She affected
not to understand what was meant by immodesty in the context:

I am sure they must be more abus'd than I think is possible (for I
have not seen the Book, nor can imagine what's in't) before they can
be render'd otherwise than Sir Edward Deering says in his Epilogue
to Pompey.

————No bolder thought can tax
Those Rimes of blemish to the blushing Sex,
As chaste the lines, as harmless is the sense,
As the first smiles of infant innocence.

So that I hope there will be no need of justifying them to Vertue and
Honour; and I am so little concern'd for the reputation of writing
Sense, that provided the World would believe me innocent of any
manner of knowledge, much less connivance at this Publication, I
shall willingly compound never to trouble them with the true Copies,
as you advise me to do: which if you still should Judge absolutely
necessary to the reparation of this misfortune, and to general satisfac-
tion; and that, as you tell me, all the rest of my friends will press me
to it, I should yield to it with the same reluctancy as I would cut off a

Limb to save my Life. However I hope you will satisfie all your acquaintance of my aversion to it, and did they know me as well as you
do, that Apology were very needless, for I am so far from expecting
applause for any thing I scribble, that I can hardly expect pardon; and
sometimes I think that employment so far above my reach, and unfit
for my Sex, that I am going to resolve against it for ever; and could I
have recovered those fugitive Papers that have escap'd my hands, I
had long since made a sacrifice of them all. The truth is, I have an in-
corrigible inclination to that folly of riming, and intending the effects
of that humour, only for my own amusement in a retir'd life; I did
not so much resist it as a wiser woman would have done; but some of
my dearest friends having found my Ballads, (for they deserve no better name) they made me so much believe they did not dislike them,
that I was betray'd to permit some Copies for their divertisement; but
this, with so little concern for them, that I have lost most of the originals, and that I suppose to be the cause of my present misfortune;
for some infernal Spirits or other have catch'd those rags of Paper,
and what the careless blotted writing kept them from understanding,
they have supplied by conjecture, till they put them into the shape
wherein you saw them, or else I know not which way it is possible
for them to be collected, or so abominably transcrib'd as I hear they
are. I believe also there are some among them that are not mine.[43]

A clue to the real reason for the suppression of *Poems* 1664 may be
found in the close of this letter, as she begs to excuse herself with 'the
worthy persons that had the ill luck of [her] converse, and so their
Names expos'd in this impression without their leave,' of whom the
most determined was the real engineer of the withdrawal, John
Jeffreys, exposed without his permission as the rejected suitor of Mary
Carne. In *Poems* 1664, Anne Owen is named in full and identified as
Lucasia; as a disappointed suitor for her hand, Sir Charles Cottrell is
unlikely to have waited until this indiscretion came to her attention
before taking action to protect her. Rosania is identified as 'Mrs M.
Aubrey,' her 'private marriage' is referred to, and she is identified in
the title of another poem as 'now Mrs Montagu'; Regina and John
Collier, and Mary Carne are named in full; Malet Stedman is named
as Mrs M. Stedman; Palaemon is identified as Francis Finch; Silvander
as Sir Edward Dering. That these identifications are accurate is itself
cause for astonishment. If we begin to ask how the unauthorized
editors could have come by them, we are faced with a very limited
number of possibilities. Marriott's compilation is not based upon rags

of paper but on a careful transcription from a collection of seventy-four poems, all of them probably in the same hand, given the uniformity of orthography and elisions. Despite a different ordering of the poems, Worcester College MS 6.13, of which Thomas knew nothing, seems a possible candidate. It lacks the same two poems as *Poems* 1664, while containing all but the last two of the rest. Like *Poems* 1664, it reads 'bounty' as 'Beauty' in one poem and accidentally drops the same line in two others.

Within months of the suppression of her book, Orinda succumbed to smallpox. At the beginning of 1667 Marriott turned all right to Orinda's poems over to his friend and colleague Henry Herringman.[44] It is not surprising then that the 1667 edition of Orinda's poems is based upon the edition of 1664. Like 1664, 1667 begins with the poems addressed to the king and members of the royal family, and follows the same order until Poem 24, when it skips two poems, which it re-incorporates in slightly different order. The same order is resumed ten poems later and maintained until after Poem 67, at which point 1667 includes two poems not before printed, before resuming the same sequence as 1664 until Poem 77, which was the last to be printed in 1664, after which forty-one additional poems are printed in no obvious sequence. Not only do the 1667 texts of the seventy-five poems agree with 1664 against the manuscripts in far more instances than they diverge, but some of the corrections of obvious corruptions in the 1664 version indicate that the 1667 editor had no more authoritative version to hand. For example, in 1664 the line:

The intermitted stormes return'd as fast

was dropped from 'On the faire weather at the Coronacon.' It was substituted in 1667 by:

The storm return'd with an impetuous hast.[45]

In 'La Grandeur d'Esprit' where the 1664 compositor had read 'company' for 'constancy' the word was corrected to 'honesty.' The new editor did not limit himself to correction of faults that had escaped in the printing of 1664. Whole couplets accurately transcribed from the original in 1664 are excised or rewritten. In 'On the numerous accesse of the English to waite upon the King in Holland,' line 4 –

As Pompey's residence made Afrique Rome –

was re-written as:

> As Pompey's camp, wher e'er it mov'd, was Rome.[46]

It is of course possible that both Dering and Polexander, whose versions agree with 1664 against 1667, were copying from that edition but on balance it seems more likely that the 1667 editor is supplying his own improvements. An awkward couplet in 'To the Queene on her arrivall at Portsmouth,'

> We did enjoy but half our King before;
> You us our prince, and him his peace restore

was dropped, while another,

> (For fortune would her wrongs to him repaire,
> By courtships greater than her mischiefes were:

was rewritten as:

> (For Fortune in amends now courts him more
> Than ever she affronted him before: ...[47]

From 'In memory of ... Mrs Mary Lloyd of Bodidrist' one couplet (lines 41–2) was dropped and another,

> She lost all sence of wrong, glad to beleive
> That it was in her power to forgive.

appears as:

> She grew to love those wrongs she did receive
> For giving her the power to Forgive.[48]

Five couplets were dropped from 'Rosania shaddow'd' and another,

> She scorns the sullen trifles of the time
> But things transcendent do her thoughts sublime;

appears as:

> Transcendent things her noble thoughts sublime
> Above the faults and trifles of the Time.[49]

As the autograph, Polexander, and Dering all agree with 1664, it is all but certain that what we have here is another of the 1667 editor's smoothings out of Philips's choppier and more interesting sense and sound. In 'A Friend' the difficult parenthesis:

> (As liquors, which asunder are the same)

becomes:

> (As a far stretch'd out River's still the same).[50]

The most astonishing of these revisions, to be found in no pre-1667 version, occurs at the end of 'Friendship' when the concluding couplet:

> Free as first agents are true friends, and kind,
> As but themselves I can no likeness find.

becomes:

> What shall I say? when we true friends are grown,
> W'are like – Alas, w'are like our selves alone.[51]

Such cases as these increase the probability that the problem with 1664 was not that it was an incorrect transcription, but that it was a transcription from an unvetted original. By contrast, the text of *Pompey*, which had been corrected before its original publication, is allowed by the 1667 editors to stand, whereas 'Horace' is extensively rewritten. As transcribed for the Rosania manuscript 'Horace' is stylistically very close to the manuscript of *Pompey*. As printed in 1667, however, Act 3, scene 6 was completely recast, more than 150 lines of the rest were rewritten, and a character's name was changed from Curiace to Curtius throughout. The recasting of Act 3, scene 6 is so far completely inexplicable.

Peter Beal, in his *Index to English Literary Manuscripts*, calls Orinda's 'one of the best documented centres of manuscript circulation in the 17th century.'[52] He finds her unusual among her contemporaries in that she left 'a substantial body of works in her own hand.'[53] Though both

No blooming youth shall ever make me err
I will the beauty of his mind prefer
If humans rites shall call me hence
It shall be with some man of sence
Not with the great but with a good estate
Not too well read nor yet illeterate in o
In all his actions moderate grave & wise
Redyer to bear than offer injuries
And in good works a constant doer
Faithfull in promise & liberall to the poor
He has being qualified is allways seen
Ready to serve his friend his country & his king
Such men as these you say there are but few
Their hard to find & I must grant it too
But if I hap to change my life
Tis only such a man shall call me wife

Humbly Dedicated too Mrs Anne Barlow

C: Fowler

The unique copy of two early poems and a paragraph of prose written in
Orinda's own hand on a single sheet of paper. National Library of Wales,
Orielton Estate MSS, Parcel 24 (by kind permission of the National Library
of Wales).

[recto] 'No blooming youth' dedicated to 'Mrs Anne Barlow' and signed 'C
Fowler.' Fowler was Orinda's maiden name; the poems must, therefore,
have been written before her marriage to Colonel James Philips in 1648.

A marry'd state affords but little Ease
The best of husbands are so hard to please
This in wifes Carefull faces you may spell
Tho they desemble their misfortunes well
A virgin state is crown'd with much content
Its allways happy as its innocent
No Blustering husbands to create yr fears
No pangs of child birth to extort yr tears
No childrens crys for to offend your ears
Few worldly crosses to distract yr prayers
Thus are you freed from all the cares that do
Attend on matrymony & a husband too
Therefore madm be advised by me
Turn turn apostate to loves Levity
Suppress wild natura if she dare rebell
Theres no such thing as leding Apes in hell

A receipt to cure a Love sick Person who cant obtain the Party desired

Take two oz of the spirits of reason three oz of the Powder of experiance five drams
of the Juce of Discretion three oz of the Powder of gold advise & a spoonf of the
Cooling water of Consideration make these all up into Pills & besure to drink a little
content after ym & then the head will be clear of maggots & whimsies & you restored to
yr right sences but the persons that wont be rule must become a sacrifise to cupid &
dye for love for all the Doctors in the world cant cure ym

if this wont do apply the plaister & if that wont do its out of my power to find
out what wel

[verso] 'A marry^d state' and 'A receipt to cure a Love sick Person who
cant obtain the Party desired.' Probably intended for Anne Barlow, these
are early examples of Orinda's attempts to make or mar matches among
her friends.

these claims are surely true, Orinda is still of the seventeenth century and a woman. Collaboration, especially among the royalist coteries of the Interregnum, was the rule. Not only did patrons of young talent assist them in refining and correcting their work, but poems were lengthened and shortened and altered as they were copied. A few lines were sometimes taken as a theme or epigraph upon which the amateur versifiers exercised their wit. Possessiveness, even with regard to invention, was bad form. Any careful collation of the commonplace books of university wits of the 1650s, for example, produces hundreds of variations of well-known works, very few of them attributed. Songs that are nowadays attributed to any of three or four authors may have been worked on by all three. It has long been known that lines to be found in Orinda's autograph can also be found embedded in longer poems in the Portland MSS.[54] A recent discovery in a manuscript miscellany of 1657–8 of three poems by Orinda in startlingly variant versions makes more urgent than ever a careful examination of the materials out of which the Orinda canon has been assembled. Orinda was told by her contemporaries that some of the poems printed as hers in 1664 were not by her. Because she never did supply the correct copies as Cottrell urged her to do, the possibility remains that she is not the sole author of the poems collected in 1664, or even of those in the autograph Tutin MS. Careful mapping of Katherine Philips's place in the web of royalist manuscript circulation during the verseless times of the Interregnum might just break up the author-shaped parcel that is Orinda into something more complex and truer to the conditions of verse composition in the Interregnum.

NOTES

1   Patrick H.B. Thomas, 'An Edition of the Poems and Letters of Katherine Philips, 1632–1665,' PhD diss., University College of Wales, Aberystwyth, 1982. *The Collected Works of Katherine Philips, the Matchless Orinda*, ed. Patrick H. B. Thomas, G. Greer, and R. Little, 3 volumes (Stump Cross: Stump Cross Books, 1990–3).

2   Peter Beal, *Index of English Literary Manuscripts*, volume 2: *1625–1700* (London: Mansell Publishing, 1993), 2: 129.

3   Beal, *Index*, 2: 128.

4   University of Texas at Austin, Harry R. Ransome Humanities Research Center, Misc. *HRC 151 Phillipps MS 14,937; Beal, *Index*, 2: 130, 'Dering MS.'

5 University of Cincinnati MS Phillipps 14,392, Shelfmark DA 447f, D4 A3 R, B.

6 Philips, *Works*, 1: 87 and 269.

7 Philips, *Works*, 1: 90 and 270.

8 Philips, *Works*, 1: 91 and 271.

9 Beal, *Index*, 2: 129.

10 Philips, *Works*, 1: 45; cf. Beal, *Index*, 2: 129.

11 Philips, *Works*, 1: 88–9 and 270.

12 See Philips, *Works*, 3: 119–92, where the text is collated with the printed version and the French original.

13 Philips, *Works*, 2: 32 (Letter IX); cf. Letter XIII of 30 July (Philips, *Works*, 2: 45):

> I have just now receiv'd the letter you directed to me at Cardigan, wherein you give me an account of their Majesty's great Goodness to me, for which I return you many Thanks, and particularly for the Alterations you made in the Poem.

As none of the poems addressed to royalty is to be found in Orinda's autograph or in a presentation copy, we have no way of knowing whether what we have are versions corrected by other hands or not. The revisions to be seen in *Poems* 1667 may or may not reflect Cottrell's 'alterations' for the original presentation copies.

14 Philips, *Works*, 2: 119; 1: 191–2 and 372–3.

15 *Pompey: A Tragoedy* (Dublin: John Crooke for Samuel Dancer, 1663).

16 Philips, *Works*, 2: 60–1.

17 Philips, *Works*, 3: 56

18 Philips, *Works*, 2: 70.

19 Orinda's memory of her own work seems to fail her here. All printed versions of these lines (*Pompey*, 5.2.7–8) read:

> If Heaven which did persecute you still,
> Had made my power equal to my will.

20 Philips, *Works*, 2: 77–8.

21 Philips, *Works*, 3: 7–8 (*Pompey*, 1.1.51–2).

22 Philips, *Works*, 3: 62 (*Pompey*, 4.2.18).

23 Philips, *Works*, 3: 31 (*Pompey*, 2.1.93–4).

24 Philips, *Works*, 2: 93.

25 Philips, *Works*, 3: 68–9.

26 Philips, *Works*, 3: 25, 26, 28, 29, 31, etc.

27 Philips, *Works*, 1: 143 and 287.

28 Philips, *Works*, 1: 87–8 and 269.

29 Philips, *Works*, 1: 90–1 and 270.

30 Philips, *Works*, 2: 88 and n3.

31 Philips, *Works*, 3: 186–8.

32 Philips, *Works*, 3: 191–5.

33 Philips, *Works*, 1: 193–5 and 302.

34 Philips, *Works*, 1: 250–1.

35 Philips, *Works*, 1: 195–6.

36 Abraham Cowley, *Verses Written upon Several Occasions* (London: Henry Herringman, 1663).

37 *The Intelligencer*, Monday, 18 January 1664.

38 Philips, *Works*, 2: 125.

39 Philips, *Works*, 2: Appendices 1, 2, and 5.

40 Philips, *Works*, 2: 142.

41 *A Transcipt of the Registers of the Worshipful Company of Stationers from 1640–1708 A.D.*, 3 volumes (London: privately printed, 1913), 2: 334, 25 November 1663.

42 Philips, *Works*, 2: 128.

43 Philips, *Works*, 2: 129–30.

44 In mid-1664 Marriott and Herringman had collaborated on the second edition of Henry King's *Poems, Elegies, Paradoxes and Sonets*, Marriott having published the first in 1657.

45 Philips, *Works*, 1: 73 and 262–3.

46 Philips, *Works*, 1: 70 and 261.

47 Philips, *Works*, 1: 74–5 and 264.

48 Philips, *Works*, 1: 113–14 and 277.

49 Philips, *Works*, 1: 118–20 and 279.

50 Philips, *Works*, 1: 168 and 295.

51 Philips, *Works*, 1: 151 and 290.

52 Beal, *Index*, 2: 133.

53 Beal, *Index*, 2: 126.

54 The juvenilia consist of two poems, one on each side of a single sheet: one, beginning 'No blooming youth shall ever make me err,' dedicated to Mrs Anne Barlow, and signed with Orinda's maiden name C. Fowler, may with reasonable certainty be attributed to Orinda. The other, which begins 'A married state affords but little ease,' presents a problem. These sixteen lines appear as part of a longer poem beginning 'Madam, I cannot but congratulate' in four manuscript versions, all of which date from the 1680s. The extract, if such it is, in Philips's hand dates from 1646–7. We shall probably never know whether a later poem simply incorporated a pre-existing passage of sixteen lines, as would not have been in the least unusual, or whether Philips copied out sixteen lines from a poem that had caught her eye, of which we have not found a surviving copy of the earlier date.

5 Julian of Norwich and Self-Textualization

I

After the first printed edition of Julian of Norwich's *A Revelation of Love* was published in 1670 by the Benedictine monk Serenus Cressy, a Church of England divine was withering in his contempt for the kind of spirituality it represented. '[D]o we,' he asked, 'publish to the world the Fanatick Revelations of distempered brains, as Mr Cressy hath very lately done ...? We have, we thank God, other ways of employing our devout retirements, than in reading such fopperies as these are.'[1] In describing the book as 'the Fanatick Revelations of distempered brains,' and in his crack about 'devout retirements,' the writer – Edward Stillingfleet, the leading anti-Roman controversialist of his day – was making play with its title: 'XVI Revelations of Divine Love shewed to a devout servant of our lord called Mother Juliana an anchorete of Norwich.' The real irony, of course, is that if Stillingfleet had read the book through to the sixty-sixth chapter, which seems unlikely, he would have discovered that the author herself believed at one stage that she had gone mad. *A Revelation of Love* describes a series of events that took place in May 1373, when the writer was thirty years old and a half and was so ill that she almost died. The priest who administered the last rites placed a crucifix at the foot of her bed and she was propped up so that she could look at it. Then began a series of 'showings' which started with her suddenly becoming aware that Christ's head had begun to bleed under the crown of thorns. Out of these showings she was to develop over many years an extended theological meditation of great subtlety and daring, as she thought through the meanings of what she had seen. After the fifteenth showing, though, her sickness and pain returned:

Thann comm a religiouse personn to me and asked me how I farde, and I sayde that I hadde raued þatday. And he lugh lowde and enterlye. And I sayde: The crosse that stode atte my bedde feete, it bled faste; and with this worde the personn that I spake to wex alle sadde and meruelande. And onn ane I was sare aschamed for my reklessenes, and I thou3t thus: this man takys it sadlye, the leste worde that I myght saye, that says na mare þerto. And when I sawe that he toke it so sadely and with so grete reuerence, I wex ryght gretly aschamed ...²

Then a religious person came to me and asked me how I was doing, and I said I had raved today. And he laughed loudly and heartily. And I said: 'The cross that stood at the foot of my bed – it bled freely.' And at these words the person that I spoke to became very solemn, marvelling. And immediately I was deeply ashamed at my heedlessness, and I thought: 'This man takes seriously the least word I say, who says no more about it.' And when I saw that he took it seriously and with such great reverence, I became very much ashamed ...

This records the originary moment of the text, a moment which reaches back to the liminal realm between living and dying, beyond or before rationality, in which whatever the visionary experience was took place. It might be expressed, in Kristevan terms, as the realm of the semiotic which precedes the symbolic order. Julian's own first word for it is 'raving.' But she is shown – or rather shows herself and her readers – first through the religious person and then through Jesus himself, that madness need not be a source of contempt or fear, but of wisdom. It is because the 'religious person' stops laughing and marvels, precisely because he does not interpret her revelations as the product of a 'distempered brain,' that she in turn re-evaluates and finds a language for what she has seen. Fourteenth-century clerical culture – unlike its seventeenth-century reformed equivalent – offers her an identity as a visionary rather than a lunatic. The re-evaluation of madness is reiterated in her final showing, which is of Jesus sitting in her soul. She hears him speak to her 'withowtyn voyce and withowten openynge of lyppes': 'Witte it welle, it was na rauynge that thowe sawe to day, botte take it and leue it, and kepe þe ther to, and þou schalle nought be ouercomenn.'³ (Understand well, it was no raving that you saw today. But take hold of it, and trust it, and adhere to it, and you shall not be overcome.)

The very process of writing these self-authorizing moments creates a new identity, more daring even than that of the visionary and presumably rarely imaginable by Englishwomen before this, that of the author of a work of spiritual guidance:

> And so ys my desyre that it schulde be to euery ilke manne the same profytte that I desyrede to my selfe, and þerto was styrryd of god in the fyrste tyme when I saw itte; for yt [ys] comonn and generale as we are all ane, and I am sekere I sawe it for the profytte of many oder.[4]

> And so it is my desire that it [the revelation] should be of the same benefit to everyone as I wanted for myself, and I was moved to that by God the first time I saw it; for it is common and general as we are all one, and I am sure I saw it for the benefit of many others.

I shall argue that the differences between the surviving texts of *A Revelation of Love* can be related to Julian's evolving sense of herself as an author under a divine imperative to write 'for the profytte of many oder.'[5] A private experience which was originally part of a personal psycho-history thus enters the public domain as a book. This is of course what happens with much writing; an unusual aspect of Julian's work is that this process is written into it. Insofar as *A Revelation of Love* records this transformation, it is a text about self-textualization.

There are two versions of *A Revelation of Love*, a short and a long (though the long survives in what I shall argue are differing states). We do not know precisely when these two versions were written, but we do know that Julian was born in 1342/3, had the visions in 1373 and died some time after 1416. The first document referring to her as an anchoress is dated 1394, when she was over fifty.[6] It has been assumed that the short version was written soon after she had the visions, but Nicholas Watson has recently proposed new and later datings for both versions.[7] These rest, however – as all the dating arguments do – on fairly slim pieces of evidence. The short version may have been produced in the later 1370s or (according to Watson) the late 1380s, and from internal evidence the long version cannot have been completed before 1393 and could have been much later than that. Watson suggests around 1413. In the short version the theology developed in the long version is only embryonic. The long version is in some ways like a series of pictures that have been partially over-painted. What Julian saw in May 1373 must have been recreated in her memory and mulled over, teased out, talked through, and then written down. This first written version – the short version – must itself have stimulated more thinking, more talking, and more writing.

The long version carries these archaeological layers within it. Some passages are taken over from the short version more or less verbatim. Others are incorporated and altered. Much of it, especially in the second half of the book, is completely new. This new writing was itself the product of a continual, rather than a finite, process. There are the famous occasions which reveal this, as at the end when Julian says: 'And fro that time that it was shewid I desired oftentimes to witten what was our Lords mening. And fifteen yer after and more I was answerid in gostly understonding ...'[8] (And from the time that it was shown, I often wanted to know what our Lord's meaning was. And more than fifteen years later, I was answered in spiritual understanding ....) In chapter fifty-one she explains that for a long time she did not know the full meaning of the vision she received of a lord and a servant until, nearly twenty years later, a voice told her to pay particular attention to all its 'propertes and condition.'[9] She describes how she focused her mind on the way the lord sat, on what clothes he was wearing, how the servant stood and so on, and bit by bit was able to move forward to unravel the complex signification of what she was looking at. There are many other places in which she describes the restless movement of mental action: blocked, released, circling round an idea, moving from uncertainty towards more confident utterance.[10]

The long version is a record of a mind in process, not just an achieved statement. It is as if I should incorporate into what I have written here the difficulties I had in working it out: the half-written drafts, the false starts, the discarded ideas, and so on. The convention with which we work is that the reader does not want to hear all that; she wants to know where I have got to, not how I got there. The conventions of the devotional handbooks of Julian's own day, like *The Chastising of God's Children* or *Contemplations of the Love and Dread of God*, were the same, and this dictates their relationship with the reader: their self-assured didactic voices have left the throes of composition far behind. These voices are quite different from the fluid identities that are recalled in the complex process of retrospection which is written into Julian's text. An evolving conception of self seems to underlie its layering, and this may relate to the circumstances of Julian's own life as well as to the circumstances of its composition. It is possible that when she had her visions in 1373 she was a laywoman; when she wrote the first version of *A Revelation of Love* she was probably not yet an anchoress, though she may have been a widowed vowess or conceivably a nun.[11] When she wrote the long version – after 1393 and possibly much later – she had entered the anchorhold at St Julian's Conesford in Norwich. Thus during the period in which the different versions were produced her identity and roles, and her place in the spiritual hierarchy, were changing.

The process of self-textualization was, as I have said, one that took many years to achieve: it entailed first giving to pre-discursive mental experience – the experience that felt like madness – verbal and then written shape, separating the inchoate and indeterminate visions (or whatever they were, for the notion of vision is itself textual) so that they could be analysed and discussed, so that the writer could cross-refer from one to the other, so that they could be listed in the contents, so that, as a book, they could become part of other people's reading. The models of the book as material object are the early manuscripts of those other late fourteenth- and early fifteenth-century works of what Watson is teaching us to call vernacular theology:[12] Hilton, the *Cloud*-author, *The Chastising of God's Children* and *Stimulus Amoris*. In many manuscripts these texts are divided, as Julian's eventually is, into chapters with chapter headings and contents lists; they are designed to be readerly, accessible, and usable. They are the products of collaboration between writers, scribes and what might be called 'clerical facilitators' of various kinds. Jerome McGann's terms are, I believe, appropriate to this kind of literary production: '[L]iterary works are fundamentally social rather than personal or psychological products, [which] do not even acquire an artistic form of being until their engagement with an audience has been determined. In order to secure such an engagement, literary works must be produced within some appropriate set of social institutions, even if it should involve but a small coterie of amateurs.'[13] This is the model of authorship which I propose for *A Revelation of Love*. We should not be misled by the popular notion of the solitary anchoress locked away in her remote cell without contact with the external world: that is a gothic creation and belongs with broken columns, hooded monks, and screech-owls. The anchorhold in St Julian's Conesford was in one of the busiest areas of Norwich. Answerable to her bishop through her parish priest, Julian was part of the ecclesiastical structure of the diocese. One of her functions was – as we know from Margery Kempe's *Book* – to provide spiritual advice. She did not live alone: we may even know the name of one of her servants, Alice.[14] When she entered the anchorhold she would have been cross-examined about her orthodoxy and her mental stamina. It is inconceivable that she could publish a book in Norwich without official sanction and, very probably, official assistance.[15]

Despite the fact that there is no evidence at all that Julian was a solitary in 1373 when she had the visions, nevertheless medieval and modern editors of *A Revelation of Love* alike have constructed their author simply as a recluse. The oldest manuscript, the Amherst manuscript of the short version, which was copied around 1450 from another copy of 1413, has preserved the latter's colophon: 'Here es a visionn schewed by the goodenes of god to a deuoute womann, and hir name es Julyan, that is recluse atte Norwyche and 3itt ys onn lyfe, anno domini millesimo CCCC xiij°'[16] (Here is a vision shown by the goodness of God to a devout woman whose name is Julian who is a recluse at Norwich and is still alive in AD 1413). The earliest complete manuscript of the long version, Paris, Bibliothèque Nationale, fonds anglais 40, which was probably copied in the first half of the seventeenth century or slightly before, concludes 'Explicit liber revelacionum Julyane anacorite Norwiche' (Here ends the book of the revelations of Julian, anchoress of Norwich). This title has been adapted by Edmund Colledge and James Walsh in the two-volume Toronto edition based on the Paris manuscript – *A Book of Showings to the Anchoress Julian of Norwich* – even though they argue in their introduction that Julian entered the anchorhold only after writing both versions of her book, twenty years after she saw the showings.[17] 'Julian the Solitary' is the title of a distinguished biographical article that in fact argues persuasively that Julian was a laywoman at the time of her visions, who might even have been married and had a child.[18] Clearly *A Book of Showings to a Young Widow* would have a very different set of resonances.

The idea of the anchoress as solitary has generated certain editorial assumptions: the isolated recluse, voluntarily walled up in her cell, seems to represent a paradigm of notions about the autonomous author as an 'isolated figure freely expressing [her] uniquely individual and privileged intention,'[19] the opposite view, that is, from that of McGann which I quoted earlier. This, of course, sounds dangerous in a woman writer, and it is interesting to see how Colledge and Walsh, who believe in the primacy of authorial intention as an editorial principle, manage both to construct the author as an isolate and keep her under control. They suggest, despite their title, that when she had her visions Julian may have been in a convent. This enables them to credit her with formidable learning, even for (or perhaps especially for) a nun: 'What is however beyond any doubt is that when young Julian had received an exceptionally good grounding in Latin, in Scripture and in the liberal arts, and that thereafter she was able and permitted to read widely in Latin and vernacular spiritual classics.'[20] This version of Julian as mistress of kinds of knowledge usually restricted in her day to male clerics is in some ways exhilarating. This is a Julian who is an answer to Chaucer's simpering and ignorant Prioress, and who has her counterparts in powerful nun-administrators of the late fourteenth and early fifteenth centuries, like Sybilla de Felton of Barking. Nevertheless entry into this particular male club brings with it its own forms of control: one of the governing impulses of Colledge and Walsh's edition is to demonstrate the orthodoxy of Julian's thought. The very extensive commentary at the foot of each page is intended to make explicit to the reader her incorporation into 'the Western monastic traditions of *lectio divina* of which she was heiress' and to which, they believe, her book is 'a great monument.'[21] All aspects of Julian's thinking, it seems, are derivative. Almost everything she writes is an echo of what she has read, and she is not granted any intellectual autonomy. Moreover, this view of Julian as steeped in the techniques of Latin rhetoric leads directly to Colledge and Walsh's choice of copy-text. The manuscript on which they base their edition – the Paris manuscript – is chosen mainly because, they claim, it preserves 'Julian's rhetorical figures, which are integral to her thought.'[22] Their treatment of the text is also driven by their under-standing of Julian's intellectual concerns: this leads them to alter a chapter division against the evidence of all the manuscripts and to redefine the starting point of a showing, confidently stating that there 'can be no doubt' about Julian's intentions.[23]

The other recent editors of the long version, Marion Glasscoe[24] and Georgia Ronan Crampton,[25] are both more cautious than Colledge and Walsh about Julian's formal learning and regard the question of whether or not she knew Latin as open. Formal rhetoric is less central to Glasscoe's conception of Julian than it is to Colledge and Walsh's, and it is different in nature. Glasscoe comments that 'the kind of rhetorical control shown in [Julian's prose] is quite consistent with an oral tradition.' She suggests that Julian may have dictated her book to an amanuensis and that the characteristics of her prose suggest 'an author thinking aloud rather than polishing pre-formulated ideas.'[26] This view of Julian leads her, and Crampton as well, to select a diffe-rent manuscript as copy-text from that chosen by Colledge and Walsh. They choose the one whose language best preserves the characteristics of fourteenth-century speech, which is London, British Library, Sloane

2499, discussed below. Glasscoe raises the possibility of Julian's deriving her learning from oral sources as well as written ones: her Julian inhabits an oral-literate culture rather than a learned, monastic one. Both of these editors – Glasscoe and Crampton – have produced editions with minimal commentaries which do not aim, as Colledge and Walsh do, to locate Julian in a particular sub-culture, but leave contextualizing to the reader.

Denise Nowakowski Baker, in a recent book on Julian's thought, mediates between these two positions. On the one hand, she argues that 'by the time Julian completed the final version sometime after 1393, she had acquired an understanding of moral and mystical theology that enabled her to use this discipline's terminology and adapt its concepts with subtle creativity.'[27] On the other hand, Baker is not convinced that Julian's knowledge of Latin devotional and theological texts is necessarily firsthand; she suggests that she may have acquired it 'through a variety of means ranging from sermons to conversations to reading.'[28] We surely hardly need to remind ourselves that 'reading' at this period does not necessarily mean private reading in silence, but is more commonly the shared, communal experience of reading aloud. Baker's positioning of Julian in the more uncontrolled oral-literate culture I have already mentioned also makes possible a view of her, not as the docile heiress of monastic *lectio divina*, but as a daring thinker whose theodicy 'implicitly challenges the Augustinian solution to the problem of evil by calling into question its fundamental premises.'[29] Baker uses only the Colledge and Walsh editions of the long and short versions in her study. In her introduction she has a brief account of the manuscripts but does not apparently regard textual issues as relevant to the argument of her book. It is surprising how little concern, on the whole, commentators on *A Revelation of Love* show about the status of the text from which they work, and Baker is no exception.

Baker's view of Julian, while not explicitly feminist, will no doubt prove attractive to feminist readers. One thing we might notice about it is that its model of authorship, like Marion Glasscoe's, is implicitly social. Glasscoe's suggestion that Julian dictated her texts to an amanuensis seems to me entirely plausible. Nicholas Watson argues against this, on the grounds that 'it is hard to imagine any (presumably clerical) amanuensis resisting the temptation to make his presence felt, as such amanuenses do in numbers of works by continental visionaries as well as in *The Book of Margery Kempe*.'[30] Amanuenses do not, of course, have to be male clerics (though I shall argue later that there is a discernible 'clerical' voice in the long version of the text). I cannot see why one of her servants, perhaps Alice – who may be the woman friend about whose spiritual welfare Julian expresses particular concern in both versions of her book – could not have at one time played this role. Using an amanuensis is not necessarily an indication of illiteracy but of class; it separates reading and composition from the manual labour of writing and frees up time for prayer, study, and meditation. In particular I think that the complex process of taking the book through the later stages of its evolution – numbering the visions and the chapters, devising the contents list, adding chapter headings, inserting cross-references – may well have been a collaborative one. The rest of my discussion is about this process.

II

I have already mentioned the sole manuscript of the short version, the Amherst manuscript – London, British Library, Additional 37790 – which is a devotional anthology compiled around 1450. There is no surviving medieval copy of a complete text of the long version. The manuscripts containing the long version all date from the seventeenth century and seem to have been copied by English recusant nuns at Cambrai and Paris. It is from these circles that Serenus Cressy is assumed to have acquired the manuscript which lies behind the 1670 print with which I began. Two of these manuscripts made by nuns are textually significant: one, written in the early seventeenth century, forms the basis, as I have said, of the Colledge and Walsh edition. This is Bibliothèque Nationale, fonds anglais 40. The other, probably slightly later in date, is British Library, Sloane 2499. A third manuscript, also in the Sloane collection (British Library, Sloane 3705), derives from the earlier Sloane one and so can be discounted for the purposes of this discussion. So also can Cressy's print of 1670 with which I began, and the former Upholland Northern Institute manuscript, containing four folios of excerpts, both of which derive, directly or indirectly, from the Paris manuscript.[31] The Paris and Sloane manuscripts contain complete but not identical texts of the long version. The main differences between them are these:

a) the language of Sloane has more northerly features than that of the Paris manuscript;
b) the Sloane manuscript has chapter headings summarizing the contents of each chapter;
c) in both manuscripts scribes have modernized the language, but this

is less frequent in Sloane than in the Paris manuscript (hence Glasscoe's and Crampton's decision to use it as their copy-text);

d) Sloane frequently lacks short passages which are included in the Paris manuscript, some of which may be not expansions in Paris but rather contractions in Sloane;

e) they occasionally disagree about where chapter divisions come;

f) there are very many, apparently minor, textual divergences, some of which have interpretative implications.[32]

The relationship between these two manuscripts is not clear, though they do not share an immediate common ancestor. I shall argue that the divergences between them may take us back to the early history of the text and perhaps to Julian's circle.

There is one other relevant manuscript which has not had much attention paid to it. This is a devotional anthology of around 1500, now owned by Westminster Cathedral, which contains excerpts from the long version, skilfully and intelligently selected and put together to make a continuous piece of prose, rather than being divided, as the other complete texts are, into chapters. The Westminster text is very short compared to the complete texts of the long version: it covers only forty folios, whereas the long version covers 175 folios in the slightly smaller Paris manuscript. It is, though, the only medieval witness to parts of the long version.[33]

No other major fourteenth-century English author is preserved in such a late manuscript tradition. There are parallels from Scotland, where it seems that many more manuscripts have been lost: for example, the earliest surviving manuscripts of Barbour's *Bruce*, composed in the 1370s, date from the late 1480s; the earliest surviving Scottish text of Henryson's *Testament of Cresseid*, composed in the late fifteenth century, is a print of 1593.[34] But the closest parallels are probably with the medieval texts in the mid-seventeenth-century Percy Folio Manuscript: for some romances Percy is the only witness. In the cases where we can compare the Percy texts with medieval versions, the extent of modernization is plain. As far as I am aware, scholars place little weight on the Percy versions precisely because they are so late. With *A Revelation of Love*, though, we have no choice but to rely on these late witnesses.

Some of the problems caused by their lateness are due to modernization. The Colledge and Walsh edition, like that of Glasscoe, is self-avowedly conservative, though I am not sure that conservatism is necessarily appropriate. Editors could probably make more use of the

Westminster manuscript to correct what often seem to be post-medieval readings. But of course the difference between early fifteenth-century and seventeenth-century English is not just that the former is more archaic; it is also unstandardized. The process whereby the different dialects of written Middle English more or less coalesced into a non-regional standard originally emanating from Chancery in the 1430s has been fully charted. *A Linguistic Atlas of Late Mediaeval English* restricts its data-base to manuscripts from before about 1450 because, after this, regional differences are much more difficult to detect. The language of the short version in the Amherst manuscript has been thoroughly analysed by Frances Beer and by Colledge and Walsh in their editions. Both show that it has more northerly features than would be expected from East Anglia.[35] These features were not, it seems, introduced by the Amherst scribe, the person who made the copy around 1450, who was a conscientious transcriber of the differing dialect features of the various texts he wrote out.[36] Thus we are faced with two possibilities: the northern features preserved in the Amherst manuscript may derive from Julian herself or her amanuensis, or they may have been introduced by a later copyist, possibly by the scribe of the 1413 version which lies behind the Amherst manuscript. There is an obvious temptation to accept the latter explanation, because the 1413 colophon, which is presumably wholly scribal in origin, has northern features and so whoever wrote it was presumably a northerner.

If the northern features in the short text were simply scribal, however – if they had been introduced into an originally East Midland text by the person who copied the 1413 version that lies behind Amherst – then we would not expect to find them also in the long version. Nevertheless there are sporadic northern vowels and words in the Paris manuscript, and unmistakable northern features in the language of Sloane.[37] Colledge and Walsh were aware of this, and they comment that 'it is remarkable how often NED states that individual words, found in [the Sloane manuscript] but not in [the Paris manuscript], survived into the sixteenth and seventeenth centuries only in the Northern and Scottish dialects.'[38] They go on to draw attention to the presence of Scottish and Northumbrian women among the recusant groups in Cambrai in the second half of the seventeenth century.[39] The inference the reader is presumably supposed to draw is that one of these women, acting as scribe, introduced the northern features into the Sloane manuscript.[40] But this putative northern scribe can just as easily support a different argument, if we suppose that the copy-text from which she worked contained northern features. Her familiarity with northern forms could explain why these northernisms were pre-served until such a late stage in the transmission of the text: she was willing to tolerate them in a way that a southern scribe might not.

To take just one example of a northern word which occurs in Sloane but not in the Paris manuscript, in chapter 15 Sloane reads 'harre' ('a dry, harre wynde') where Paris has 'sharp.' Colledge and Walsh say that 'probably the P[aris] reading, *sharp*, is what Julian wrote,'[41] but only – as far as I can see – because they have already assumed that Julian probably 'spoke and composed in the North-East Midland dia-lect of Norwich.'[42] Both 'harre' and 'sharp' are northern words, and therefore a northern scribe would not have needed to emend 'sharp' to 'harre' to make the text understood. But since only 'sharp' (and not 'harre') is also southern, it looks as if the Paris manuscript's 'sharp' is an emendation of 'harre' by a scribe producing a text for a non-northern readership. The fact that there are very few northern features in the Paris manuscript may tell us nothing more than that it derives from a late fifteenth-century copy in which the language has been standardized, a manuscript – in its linguistic features – very like the Westminster manuscript. And the fact that Sloane preserves older forms of the language, as well as some northern features, suggests that it derives from an earlier fifteenth-century manuscript made before the spread of Chancery Standard obliterated regional differences, that is, before 1450 or thereabouts. The northern forms in Sloane are more significant, therefore, than their absence in Paris: they may have entered both the short and long versions at an early stage, and may take us to Julian's own circle.

It would seem to follow from this that Julian or her amanuensis, or both, spoke northern English.[43] It is usually argued that Julian spoke and wrote in the dialect of East Anglia, on the assumption, for which there is no evidence, that she was East Anglian born and bred. But if Julian was a widow, as Sister Benedicta has argued, she might have moved to East Anglia from Lincolnshire or Yorkshire on her marriage. Late-medieval towns were full of immigrants. That Julian's amanuensis was a member of her household who had made the same journey does not seem implausible. It is possible, therefore, to suggest that both the author and her amanuensis may have spoken and written in the north-erly dialect which has been preserved in the Amherst manuscript and less consistently in Sloane. A contemporary parallel would be with British Library, Cotton Nero A.X (the *Gawain and the Green Knight* manuscript), in which the dialect of the scribe is virtually identical to that of the poet, though they are clearly not the same person. The amanuensis could even be the scribe who produced the 1413 copy that lies behind the Amherst manuscript, who knew that Julian was still living in Norwich as an anchoress. I have already said that I think the process of creating a book should be seen as collaborative. I shall now turn to the numbering of showings and chapters in order to explore this further.

In the Amherst manuscript the short text appears as a continuous piece of writing, divided into twenty-five segments by large rubricated initials (I do not call these segments 'chapters' for reasons which will become clear). In their editions of the short version, Colledge and Walsh and Frances Beer have interpreted these initials as chapter markers, and have inserted numbered breaks in the text: Colledge and Walsh in fact call the divisions 'chapter i,' 'chapter ii,' and so on, and they start each new chapter on a new page. This editorial practice obscures an important difference between the short and long versions: in both the Paris and Sloane manuscripts of the latter, the text is divided into eighty-six numbered chapters, with a heading at the beginning of each chapter specifying which number it is. Another difference is that in the long version the showings are also separated out and numbered, whereas in the short version they are not. Julian does tell us in the short version that the first showing is the first: 'In this fyrste schewynge of oure lorde I sawe sex thynges in myne vndyrstandynge';[44] and a little later: 'And alle thynge oure lorde schewyd me in the fyrst syght, and gafe me space and tyme to behalde it.'[45] But from then on the whole visionary experience is rendered as a more or less inchoate sequence and the only ordering principle is temporal: 'And aftyr this,' 'And anon after,' and so on. There is no clear sense of exactly how many showings there are; nowhere in the short version does Julian say that there are sixteen.[46]

This is because the showings are not like the dreams in, say, *Piers Plowman*. There the boundaries, even when a dream is within a dream, are clearly demarcated by the dreamer's falling asleep. They structure the narrative. Julian's waking dreams seep into one another, and the long version records her own hesitation over the status of what she saw. Of the second showing, which is of Christ's discolouring, she says that she 'was sum time in doute whither it was a shewing' because it was 'so low and so litil and so simple.'[47] This passage is not in the short version, and the doubt itself seems to have been generated by the processes of rewriting and expansion which obliged her to take decisions on matters which the short version had left open. There is something arbitrary about the divisions between showings that are produced in the long version; it is often difficult to see why one showing should end where it does and another begin. It is also difficult to see why passages like, for example, the revelation in the first showing of the thing the size of a hazelnut in the palm of her hand which is all that is made, or the sensation recorded in the second showing of being at the bottom of the sea, do not constitute separate revelations, but instead are apparently parts or expansions of showings. So the process of numbering the showings was itself a complex one, and I shall return to it shortly.

First, though, I want to consider what the segments of text marked off by the rubricated initials in the Amherst manuscript are. I do not call them chapters because I take chapters to be sequentially numbered segments of text: chapter one, chapter two, and so on, and these are not numbered. They do not necessarily signal the beginning of a new showing: in fact only eight of them do. Nor does one showing go with one segment. The first showing is described in segment three; the second, third, fourth and fifth in segment eight; the sixth and seventh in segment nine; the eighth in segment ten; the ninth in segment twelve; the tenth, eleventh, twelfth, and thirteenth in segment thirteen; the fourteenth in segment nineteen; the fifteenth in segment twenty; and the sixteenth in segment twenty-two. Clearly in the short version the showings are not used as a primary means of organizing the text. So what sorts of units are the twenty-five segments? They are all short; the longest is the thirteenth which occupies folios 105^v to 106^v in the Amherst manuscript. They may well not be authorial in the narrow sense at all. On the other hand, they possibly preserve the compositional moment. Whether in the original process of dictation to a scribe, or of writing her own text, Julian may have worked in short stints. It is likely that the first draft was made on wax tablets before being transferred to expensive parchment, and so it may be that the segments I have been discussing in the short version represent the amount of text that a set of wax tablets could hold.[48]

When she came to rewrite the short version Julian must have decided at an early stage to divide its inchoate sequence into sixteen showings, and the segments of text, greatly expanded in number, became numbered chapters. The chapters, with the exception of the fifty-first, remain short and may again represent working stints. The sixteen showings, though, provide the primary means of structuring the text. They are listed and summarized in the contents list in the opening chapter of the long version in both the Paris and Sloane manuscripts. In the Paris manuscript this begins: 'Here begynneth the first chapter. This is a reuelacion of louve that Jhesu Christ our endles blisse made in xvi shewynges.'[49] The showings are also numbered in the headings of the chapters in which they begin; that is, the beginning of chapter twenty-six, for example, is headed in the Paris manuscript: 'The xij Reuelation and þe xxvj Chapter.'[50] The Sloane manuscript reads, more expansively: 'The twelfth Revelation is that the Lord our God is al sovereyn beyng. Twenty-sixth chapter.'[51] (I shall discuss the expanded chapter headings in Sloane shortly.) Nevertheless, although the showings are numbered in the chapter headings, they are not, apart from the first, fifteenth, and sixteenth showings, numbered within the text itself.[52] This means that the chapter headings must always have been integral to the long version's numerical organization; in fact, putting in numbered chapter headings makes organization possible. Without them, the reader – and the subsequent editors – could not be certain which of the sixteen showings had been reached, as is the case in the short version, nor where a particular showing begins and ends.

The numbering of the showings must have taken place before the compilation of the contents list which forms the first chapter in the Paris and Sloane manuscripts. Colledge and Walsh argue that this contents list relates to an intermediate stage of the long version, because it does not mention the parable of the lord and the servant, to which I have already alluded and which is part of showing fourteen. This parable is not in the short version and Julian tells us that she only came to understand the meaning of it 'twenty yeres after the tyme of the shewing, save three monethis,'[53] that is, early in 1388. Thus the contents list was apparently compiled after the short version was finished, but before Julian had developed the parable of the lord and the servant. Although this does show, as I have already suggested, that the process by which the long version came into being was complex, I do not agree that it is necessarily evidence of an intermediate stage in Colledge and Walsh's sense. The absence of the parable of the lord and the servant from the contents list may have another explanation.

When she came to write the long version Julian presumably worked from a marked-up copy of the short text, in which the showings had been numbered and the point at which each began and ended had been made clear. Clarifying this aspect of the short text was presumably one of the first steps undertaken in the process of revision and amplification. Julian possibly made a list of the showings as the starting-point for her expansion of the text, and this list may have become the contents list which appears as the first chapter in the Paris and Sloane manuscripts. My reason for suggesting this is that there is nothing, so far as I can see, in the contents list in the long version that could not have come from the short version. (The omission of the lord and servant parable simply confirms this.) So it looks as if the contents list was not written after, but before, the long version had been completed. It was, as I say, the starting-point for the long version, not the finish. As the long version accreted in the way I described earlier, Julian never went back to this list and rewrote it. She did not do this because she did not need to: the main structuring device of sixteen showings remained unchanged. Once she had identified the sixteen, it did not matter that the fourteenth became much more elaborate than she had originally conceived of it as being, or that the contents list referred to her initial conception of it and not her final one.

Numbering the showings enabled Julian to cross-refer between them as she expanded the text, in a way she had not been able to do in the short version. There she sometimes foreshadows her own discussion: ' ... as y schalle telle aftyr warde,'[54] 'Alle this that I hafe nowe sayde, and mare that I schalle saye eftyr ... ';[55] nevertheless, the elaborate 'recursive structure' of the long version (the term is Denise Nowakowski Baker's) depends on the numbering system. What Baker is pointing to is the element of repetition or doubling back in the long version; the way it circles round an idea, picks it up and echoes it. Cross-referring enables Julian to look both forwards and back: for example, in chapter ten, discussing the second showing, she says 'Of this it is spoken in the eighth Revelation where it tretith more of the same likenes,'[56] and at chapter thirty-five, dealing with the thirteenth showing, she says 'And the grounde of this was shewid in the first and more openly in the third, wher it seyth I saw God in a peynte [point].'[57] The forward references are more significant than the retrospective ones if we want to understand how the text was built up. Clearly Julian must have had some version of the whole work to hand in order to know what she was going to say. It is unlikely that these forward references were added later, when the long version was complete, because all of them are to passages which are also in the short version. The simplest explanation is, as I have already suggested, that she worked, initially at least, from a marked-up copy of the latter, in which the visions had been numbered and their overall structure made clear. Presumably she very soon had this structure in her head.

Although the cross-references are most frequently to showings, there is also some cross-referring to chapters. An example occurs in chapter seventeen: 'I saw in Criste a doble threst [thirst], one bodely, another gostly, the which I shall speke of in the thirty-first chapter.'[58] This is from the Sloane manuscript; the Paris manuscript just says, more vaguely, 'as I shalle sey after.'[59] But the reverse happens in chapter ten, where the Paris manuscript reads 'Of this it spekyth in the secounde reuelation in the xvj chapter'[60] ('secounde' is an error for 'viij' but the chapter reference is correct), while the Sloane manuscript reads simply 'Of this it is spoken in the eighth Revelation,'[61] without referring to the chapter. Unlike the cross-references to showings, these cross-references to chapters must have been written when the long text was complete, because it would presumably not have been possible to refer ahead to the thirty-first chapter before that chapter had been written.[62] These cross-references cannot come from the short version (unlike the cross-references to showings), because that does not have chapters. Even if we regard the segments marked off by rubrics as chapters, the cross-references do not work. They may well have been added by scribes who diligently tracked down what had possibly been left as generalized forward allusions ('as I shall sey after' and 'Of this it is spoken in the viii revelation'). If this is the case, the scribes are responding to and participating in the impulse that lies behind the division into numbered showings and chapters. They are facilitating the process which has already been started, and which had its point of origin in the aim to write 'for the profytte of many oder [others].'

There is, though, a further editorial stage to be considered. I have already mentioned that in the Sloane manuscript each of the eighty-six chapters has a heading, giving a brief summary of what it contains. These headings are often regarded as scribal or editorial. In my view, and given the kind of collaborative publication for which I am arguing, that is not on its own grounds for giving them lesser status. The language of the Sloane chapter-headings is medieval and they preserve some of the dialect features that are found in varying degrees in all the manuscripts. Nicholas Watson has pointed out that they 'are strikingly more accurate and informative than such rubrics tend to be.'[63] There seems no reason why they should not belong to a different stage in the evolving authorial/editorial process from that represented by the Paris manuscript. They belong to the most fully developed sense of the revelation as a book: at one point the Sloane text in fact refers to 'al the hole revelation from the begynnyng to the end, that is to sey, of this boke.'[64] The Paris text omits this.

In the body of the text the speaker almost always refers to herself as 'I' ('I saw,' 'I understode,' and so on). In the Sloane chapter headings, however, she is referred to in the third person. The heading of chapter eighty-one, for example, reads: 'This blissid woman saw God in dyvers manners, but she saw Him take no resting place but in manys soule,' though the chapter itself has: 'Our good Lord shewid Him in dyvers manners ... but I saw Him take no place but in mannys soule.'[65] This shift from first person to third is conventional: it also happens in the chapter headings of *The Cloud of Unknowing*, for example. There the summary of the nineteenth chapter begins: 'A schort excusacion of him þat maad þis book ...' (a brief defence of him who made this book) though the chapter itself begins: 'Som myȝt þink þat I do litil worship [honour] to Martha ...'[66] The same apparent self-approbation as we find in 'this blissid woman' also occurs in chapter headings in *The Cloud*: 'A good declaryng [explanation] of certeyn doutes ...';[67] 'A good teching how a man schal flee þees disseites [these deceits] ...'[68] The shift from first person to third only seems to be problematic when the writer is a woman.

The heading of chapter sixty-six, which is the one in which she describes how she thought that she had been raving when she saw the crucifix bleed, reads thus: 'of hir frelty and morning in disese and lyte speking after the gret comfort of Jesus, seying she had ravid; which, being hir gret sekenes, I suppose was but venial synne' (of her frailty and mourning in pain and her careless talk after the great comfort of Jesus, saying she had gone mad; which, given her serious illness, I believe was only venial sin).[69] If Julian is in the third person, who is the 'I' here? It seems to be an editorial rather than an authorial subject, and there seems to be a change of gender as well. The editorial voice, we realize, sounds masculine and clerical, able to draw nice distinctions about the gradations of sin and knowing a blessed woman when he sees one. We have no way of knowing whether or not Julian wrote the chapter headings herself, or whether they were, in fact, added by a male cleric. From my point of view it does not matter: the presence of this 'clerical' voice is only a further stage in the gradual process of textualization which began with Julian's sense that the visions were not hers alone. The Sloane manuscript is the last surviving phase of this process, and it presents Julian-in-the-text in dual form, as subject and as object. The masculine discourse which constructs Julian-as-object also enables Julian-as-subject, the visionary agent, to secure an audience. The voice that records a woman's private, fluid, exploratory, struggling, uncompletable mental experience is fixed, made public, given shape, by the masculine editorial voice speaking from its position of clerical authority, by the finite text, by the division into chapters and the grid of cross-references: in short, by its textualization. Each is necessary to the other. The process is not solitary but social, not isolated but collaborative. The anchorhold is part of the parish and the town.

NOTES

1   Quoted by Georgia Ronan Crampton in her edition of *The Shewings of Julian of Norwich* (Kalamazoo: Medieval Institute Publications, 1994), 17, from T.A. Birrell, 'English Catholic Mystics in Non-Catholic Circles,' *The Downside Review* 94 (1976): 60–81, 99–117, 213–31, at 78. Edward Stillingfleet (1635–99) was a popular and learned London preacher who became bishop of Worcester in 1689.

2   This passage is from the earlier, short version of the text, but is preserved in very similar form in the long version. See *A Book of Showings to the Anchoress Julian of Norwich*, ed. Edmund Colledge, OSA, and James Walsh, SJ, Studies and Texts 35, 2 volumes (Toronto: Pontifical Institute of Mediaeval Studies, 1978), 1: 266 and 2: 632–3, which contains both short and long versions. All quotations from the short version are from this edition unless otherwise specified. The short version has also been edited by Frances Beer, *Julian of Norwich's Revelations of Divine Love: The Shorter Version ed. from B.L. Add. MS 37790*, Middle English Texts 8 (Heidelberg: Carl Winter, 1978). Quotations from the long version are from the editions of Crampton (see n1) or Colledge and Walsh, depending on the manuscript under discussion. In this article I have used the title given to the book by Marion Glasscoe in her edition of the long version (*Julian of Norwich, A Revelation of Love* [Exeter: University of Exeter Press, 1976, rev. 1993]), in preference to the plural forms used by other editors, because Julian seems to have understood her visionary experience as one. All translations are mine.

3   *Showings*, ed. Colledge and Walsh, 1: 269 and 2: 645–6.

4   *Showings*, ed. Colledge and Walsh, 1: 220. This passage in the short version is expanded in the long into a more general meditation on inclusiveness.

5   Lynn Staley Johnson has argued that 'the long text testifies to her growing understanding of herself as a writer'; see 'The Trope of the Scribe and the Question of Literary Authority in the Works of Julian of Norwich and Margery Kempe,' *Speculum* 66 (1991): 820–38, at 833. Although my views are close to Johnson's at some points, she is not concerned with the evidence of the manuscripts, and uses only the Paris text of the long version.

6 This is the will of Roger Reed, rector of St Michael's Coslany, Norwich, who left her 2s. (Norwich Consistory Court, Reg. Harsyk, fol. 194ᵛ; cited *Showings*, ed. Colledge and Walsh, 1: 33, n68).

7 Nicholas Watson, 'The Composition of Julian of Norwich's *Revelation of Love*,' *Speculum* 68 (1993): 637–83.

8 *Shewings*, ed. Crampton, 155.

9 *Shewings*, ed. Crampton, 103.

10 See, for example, chapter 48.

11 Nicholas Watson argues that the short version is 'clearly written by a professional religious ... at one point directly appealing to Christians in contemplative life: "Of this [i.e., the insignificance of the world] nedes ilke man & woman to hafe knawynge that desyres to lyeve contemplatyfelye ... For this es the cause why thaye þat er occupyede wylfullye in erthelye besynes ... er nought he[syd] of [t]his in herte and in sawlle" (*Revelations*, ed. Beer, 45.9–15).' Watson comments that 'if "contemplatyfely" here does not refer to the *vita contemplativa* in the professional sense, it is hard to see why [the long version] ... omits the term'; see Watson, 'Composition,' 673–4, n86. But there is no guarantee that the omission in the long text is authorial, and elsewhere in the short version Julian is clearly addressing all her 'evyn cristene': see, for example, the beginning of 'chapter' VI [*Revelations*, ed. Beer, 46]. *The Abbey of the Holy Ghost* was translated in the fourteenth century for those who desired to live the religious life and yet were obliged to remain in the world.

12 See Nicholas Watson, 'Censorship and Cultural Change in Late-Medieval England: Vernacular Theology, the Oxford Translation Debate, and Arundel's Constitutions of 1409,' *Speculum* 70 (1995): 822–64.

13 Jerome McGann, *A Critique of Modern Textual Criticism* (Chicago: University of Chicago Press, 1983), 43–4.

14 See Norman P. Tanner, *The Church in Late Medieval Norwich 1370–1532*, Studies and Texts 66 (Toronto: Pontifical Institute of Mediaeval Studies, 1984), 202 and n55.

15 One long-version manuscript, London, British Library, Sloane 2499, has an explicit which is apparently early, although it has none of the northern features I discuss below. It looks like an *imprimatur* of some kind, and begins: 'I pray Almyty God that this booke com not but to the hands of them that will be His faithfull lovers, and to those that will submit them to the feith of Holy Church, and obey the holesom understondying and teching of the men that be of vertuous life, sadde age 5 and profound lerning' (*Shewings*, ed. Crampton, 15).

16 *Showings*, ed. Colledge and Walsh, 1: 201. This colophon does not, of course, claim that Julian was an anchoress at the time of the visions or at the time of writing. Nevertheless it has been a powerful influence in the construction of her authorial identity.

17 *Showings*, ed. Colledge and Walsh, 1: 43.

18 See Sister Benedicta [Ward], 'Julian the Solitary,' in *Julian Reconsidered*, ed. Kenneth Leech and Sister Benedicta (Oxford: SLG Press, 1988), 11–31.

19 See Steven Mailloux, *Interpretive Conventions: The Reader in the Study of American Fiction* (Ithaca: Cornell University Press, 1982), 107. This is not Mailloux's own position: he develops a theory of literary authorship as 'socially constituted,' in the sense that it is 'a convention-governed role that individuals can take on,' which is somewhat different from the social authorship I am arguing for here.

20 *Showings*, ed. Colledge and Walsh, 1: 44. Their argument that Julian might have had access to the library of the Austin Friars 'across the lane from [her] anchorhold' (39) does not square with their belief that she was a nun, possibly at Carrow outside Norwich, when she wrote her book. Their evidence about the intellectual life of fifteenth-century Norwich is not relevant to Julian, either, if their arguments for a date of composition before 1394 are to be accepted.

21 *Showings*, ed. Colledge and Walsh, 1: 45.

22 *Showings*, ed. Colledge and Walsh, 1: 26.

23 *Showings*, ed. Colledge and Walsh, 1: 95–7, at 95.

24 See note 2 for details.

25 See note 1 for details.

26 *Revelation of Love*, ed. Glasscoe, xviii.

27 Denise Nowakowski Baker, *Julian of Norwich's Showings: From Vision to Book* (Princeton: Princeton University Press, 1994), 12–13.

28 Baker, *Vision to Book*, 13–14.

29 Baker, *Vision to Book*, 68.

30 Nicholas Watson, 'Composition,' 674, n87.

31 See H.W. Owen, 'The Upholland Anthology: An Augustine Baker Manuscript,' *The Downside Review* 107 (1989): 274–92; Marion Glasscoe, 'Visions and Revisions: A Further Look at the Manuscripts of Julian of Norwich,' *Studies in Bibliography* 42 (1989): 103–20, at 105–6; and *Showings*, ed. Colledge and Walsh, 1: 8–9, for the manuscript formerly in possession of the Upholland Northern Institute (previously St Joseph's College, Upholland, Lancs.). This is an anthology of spiritual writings prepared by Augustine Baker for the Cambrai nuns, which contains four folios of modernized excerpts from the twelfth and

thirteenth showings of *A Revelation of Love*. The text seems to derive either from the Paris manuscript, or from that manuscript via the 1670 print.

32 These have been closely studied in Glasscoe, 'Visions and Revisions,' *passim*.

33 Editors disagree over its relation to the later manuscripts: Frances Beer and Fathers Colledge and Walsh believe that the Westminster manuscript shares an ancestor with Sloane (*Showings*, ed. Colledge and Walsh, 1: 27), while Marion Glasscoe, who edited the long text from Sloane, says that 'in the main' Westminster follows Paris and not Sloane ('Visions and Revisions,' ed. Glasscoe, 106). Georgia Ronan Crampton, who has also used the Sloane manuscript as her copy-text, takes a position between these; she agrees with Beer and with Colledge and Walsh that the Westminster text is 'in some respects closer to the Sloane texts than to [Paris]' but notes that 'it includes a brief passage which does not appear in them, but does in [Paris]' (*Shewings*, ed. Crampton, 21). I suggested a few years ago that the reason that there are no surviving fifteenth-century manuscripts of the long version, and only one of the short, is that Julian's work was suppressed in the anti-Lollard climate of the fifteenth century. I now take a different view; an analysis of the relations between the four surviving manuscripts of *A Revelation of Love* under discussion shows that before 1500 there must have been, at an absolute minimum, at least two or three copies of the short version and five or six of the long, in addition to the Amherst and Westminster manuscripts, in order to account for the ones we have today. The book may well have reached the lay-people – Julian's 'evyn cristene' – for whom it was intended. The fact that the manuscripts that have survived are the ones that were owned by clerics is not necessarily, as I used to think, evidence that the book was kept out of the hands of laypeople. It simply shows that books have a greater chance of surviving in an institutional context than in a household one. The Amherst manuscript of the short version was owned in the early sixteenth century by the Carthusian James Grenehalgh, while the Paris and Sloane manuscripts were, as I have already said, produced by nuns. See my '"Women Talking About the Things of God': A Late Medieval Sub-Culture,' in *Women and Literature in Britain, 1150–1500*, ed. Carol M. Meale (Cambridge: Cambridge University Press, 1993), 104–27.

While the present volume was in production, a critical edition of the Westminster manuscript appeared. See Julian of Norwich, 'The Westminster Text of *A Revelation of Love*,' ed. Hugh Kempster, *Mystics Quarterly* 23 (1997): 177–245.

34 This is the Charteris print of 1593. An earlier, heavily anglicized version is included in Thynne's 1532 print of Chaucer, to whom it is attributed. For discussion, see *The Poems of Robert Henryson*, ed. Denton Fox (Oxford: Clarendon Press, 1981), xciv–cii.

35 *Revelations*, ed. Beer 14–20; *Showings*, ed. Colledge and Walsh, 1: 28–32.

36 See *Revelations*, ed. Beer, 19–20. Beer analyses texts by seven different authors in the Amherst manuscript to show that the 'Amherst scribe has laboured to preserve the dialect of each of his exemplars.'

37 I disagree with Beer (*Revelations*, 18), who says there are no northern features in the long version manuscripts. Paris preserves, for example, northern 'abone' (= above; *Showings*, ed. Colledge and Walsh, 2: 621). Among northern features in Sloane not also in Paris, are: iv: 43.141, 'mare' (P = 'more'); xvi: 59.598, 'harre' (P = 'sharp'); lxxiii: 140.2981, 'slaith' (P = 'slouth'); lxxix: 148.3232, 'alsa,' (P = 'also'); lxxx: 150.3285, 'slawth' (P = 'slowth'). Chapter (roman numerals), page and line references are to Crampton's edition. The present participle in '-and' occurs frequently in Sloane, in the chapter headings as well as in the text. This feature is found sporadically in Middle English in Norfolk, however, as well as more consistently in the north. Thus although its occurrence in Sloane is evidence that this manuscript preserves forms that have been modernized in Paris, it is not unambiguous evidence of Sloane's 'northernness.' For distribution of '-and,' see *A Linguistic Atlas of Late Mediaeval English*, ed. Angus McIntosh, M.L. Samuels, and Michael Benskin, 4 volumes (Aberdeen: Aberdeen University Press, 1986), 2: 237–42.

38 *Showings*, ed. Colledge and Walsh, 1: 28

39 The 'second half of the seventeenth century' sounds rather too late for Sloane 2499, which is usually dated 1650 or earlier. Thus this argument does not really address the language issue.

40 Mother Clementina Cary, whose hand, according to *Showings*, ed. Colledge and Walsh, 1: 8, resembles that of Sloane 2499, came from a midlands, not northern, family. She was the daughter of Sir Henry Cary, a Hertfordshire knight, and his wife, Catherine Knevet of Oxfordshire.

41 *Showings*, ed. Colledge and Walsh, 2: 358.

42 *Showings*, ed. Colledge and Walsh, 1: 28.

43 This suggestion has also been made by E.I. Watkin, *On Julian of Norwich and In Defence of Margery Kempe*, 2nd ed. (Exeter: University of Exeter Press, 1979), 3.

44 *Showings*, ed. Colledge and Walsh, 1: 217

45 *Showings*, ed. Colledge and Walsh, 1: 218.

46 When Frances Beer helpfully numbered the showings in her edition of the short version, she could only do this by working backwards, so to speak, from the long version.

47 *Shewings*, ed. Crampton, 51.

48 See Michelle Brown, 'The Role of the Wax Tablet in Medieval Literacy: A Reconsideration in Light of a Recent Find from York,' *The British Library Journal* 20 (1994): 1–16.

49 *Showings*, ed. Colledge and Walsh, 2: 281. The Sloane manuscript adds 'or Revelations particular'; *Shewings*, ed. Crampton, 37.

50 *Showings*, ed. Colledge and Walsh, 2: 402.

51 *Shewings*, ed. Crampton, 71.

52 In chapter 6, revelation 1, Julian says 'For the strength and the ground of all was shewed in the first sight' (46). At the end of chapter 65 Julian says: 'Now have I told you of fifteen Revelations ... ' (131), and at the beginning of chapter 66 she says 'And after this the good Lord shewid the sixteen on the night folowing ... ' (132). Page references are to Crampton's edition.

53 *Shewings*, ed. Crampton, 103.

54 *Showings*, ed. Colledge and Walsh, 1: 226.

55 *Showings*, ed. Colledge and Walsh, 1: 252.

56 *Shewings*, ed. Crampton, 52.

57 *Shewings*, ed. Crampton, 80.

58 *Shewings*, ed. Crampton, 60.

59 *Showings*, ed. Colledge and Walsh, 2: 360.

60 *Showings*, ed. Colledge and Walsh, 2: 331.

61 *Shewings*, ed. Crampton, 52.

62 Unless a detailed plan of the chapters had been worked out in advance. The recursive and accumulative mode of composition suggests that this is unlikely, however.

63 Watson, 'Composition,' 670, n79.

64 *Shewings*, ed. Crampton, 103.

65 *Shewings*, ed. Crampton, 150.

66 *The Cloud of Unknowing*, ed. Phyllis Hodgson, EETS OS 218 (London: Oxford University Press, 1944), 5 and 49.

67 *Cloud of Unknowing*, ed. Hodgson, 4.

68 *Cloud of Unknowing*, ed. Hodgson, 8.

69 *Shewings*, ed. Crampton, 132.

6   Response

I am most pleased and flattered to be here at the conference on 'Editing Women' – with a bunch of editing women. I am also honoured because all the speakers whom you have heard have been contributors in an important way to rearranging what we call 'the canon.' These are editors fresh from the field, not without dust and heat. They have worked, or indeed are working, in neglected areas and with authors often forgotten or – more tantalizing, more infuriating – misremembered. All of these speakers have proved themselves by the contributions they have made – genuine contributions to our knowledge. Isobel Grundy has long been famous for making Lady Mary Wortley Montagu freshly famous – and freshly fresh. Isobel Grundy is still working on Montagu, and I look forward to seeing the *Romance Writings*. And who that works in the eighteenth century has not consulted the new Montagu *Letters*? Germaine Greer, that proverbial creature who 'needs no introduction,' has brought us into a new knowledge of seventeenth-century women poets in *Kissing the Rod*.[1] Now, in *Slip-Shod Sibyls*, she gives us her account, devastating as usual, of the uses and abuses of women writers who wrote or attempted to write poetry.[2] In undertaking her study, Greer is not content with accepting long-published sources, nor even all the new ones. Instead, she goes back into the manuscript and makes us interested in what she finds there.

Naomi Black, a political scientist, is editing Virginia Woolf's *Three Guineas* as a political scientist, and not as a literary type. This is all the more interesting as Woolf has sometimes been smothered with a rather suspect and elaborate literariness, and her classification as a Modern writer – or a High Modern writer – makes it easy to do this, so the political Woolf can be ignored. But *Three Guineas* is not a safe or pretty or literary text. As Black shows, it comes out of various kinds of work, in several forms. It is most truly literary where it is most disconcerting. Black demonstrates how Woolf uses common decorative matter, the letter, the photograph, fictionalizing it to make the irony of her diatribe work. *Three Guineas* is an attack upon nothing less than property, which must make the editor wary of looking at it as a property. It also has the ironic characteristic of repudiating the editor's success in advance; we are told to despise honours, awards, fame and any jingles after the name, or highly ornamented pots.

Going back deeper in time Felicity Riddy of York University tells us about Julian of Norwich, a woman writer who is even more difficult to deal with, not because she has mere literary eminence but because a kind of sainthood has been attached to her. Riddy shows that we should not think of Julian as a pious hermit of the forest. The anchoress was part of a community and her writing was a conscious enterprise. To dismiss her into the realm of visionary unconsciousness is one way of getting rid of her. Or, Riddy suggests, she becomes too independent, 'a paradigm of notions about the autonomous author,' which 'sounds dangerous in a woman writer.'[3] Riddy shows how earlier editors have constructed her as an author and suggests that seeing the two variants of Julian's description of a vision may help us to see Julian's description of a mind in action as well. I particularly like Riddy's assertion that 'The long version is a record of a mind in process, not just an achieved statement.'[4]

It seems a running theme of our symposium that the traditional editorial authorizing of women – when it has approved them at all as textual exponents – has tended to recreate them as authorial unified statements. Editors and commentators (usually male) when not getting rid of women authors, hiding them under various rugs, have tended (even if not very consciously) to take the singular woman in hand, to tidy her up and interpret her. The evidence of these talks suggests that women writers do not like being got rid of. And they may not like being made quite so tidy. Are women writers, then, a race of *Through the Looking-Glass* White Queens, quietly resistant to tucking and combing? They resist both banishment and tidying, even when they are aware, like Lady Mary, of how prudent it is for them to bow to familial or class notions of standards, and to give way before too much disapproval. The story is a sad one, for we have watched each writer getting 'framed' in a certain way. Indeed, nobody perhaps ever was or is more *framed* than the woman writer. Nature has framed her, and Nature would seem, so the cultural story has run, not to have intended at all that she should write – and least of all that she should write poetry. Germaine Greer has dealt with the problem of the woman cast forever as Muse, but not to be spoken to by the Muse. The woman writer is a poor imitator, according to that story, of the beMused man. The woman writer, however, might be aMused at all these carryings-on – yet still unwilling, or half unwilling, to drift into the void.

Unexpectedly, I found the most moving of these talks (reading them in advance) to be that by my old friend and umquhile colleague Joan Coldwell on Anne Wilkinson. It seemed particularly poignant because the story is so recent; in my own lifetime, Wilkinson wrote and died. When we hear Isobel Grundy or Germaine Greer or certainly Felicity Riddy we can comfort ourselves that their subjects were alive in long, long ago olden times, or at least in a less 'enlightened' era than our own. The story of Wilkinson shows us that nothing has changed with the changing of the centuries. The same old pattern that Germaine Greer among others long taught us to look for comes up again. A woman poet or artist is admired, fêted even, during her own time. She is published or reproduced, widely discussed and known – and then vanishes from the scene. It is almost as if she had never been, save for the occasional condescending mark of erudition in a footnote. She Also Ran.

There are certain well-known techniques of control of the woman artist, including expressed physical admiration, lover-likeness, and pseudo-gallantry. These techniques of social capture and restraint that made it hard for a woman writer of poetry to move within the literary world in the time of Aphra Behn or Katherine Philips were applied with a few elegant new variations in the Canada of the 1950s. The woman writer is her body, as Coldwell points out: 'Another [male mentor] writes of the "beautiful smile that comes into your eyes, and it is of them I am reminded on reading your verse."' As Coldwell adds, 'What may happen with such conflation is that once the body is gone, the poetry may be forgotten also.'[5]

Each of these editors and commentators has seen how much her subject wished to write. Each has felt some desire to acknowledge her subject's own desire for fame (if that unsatisfactory word will do), for influence, for readers. Many of our speakers have emphasized to us that the women writers they work on *wanted* to be published. This is so even when the writers very specifically and overtly had to act an appropriate and ladylike role in explicitly stating a desire *not* to be published. This is the case with Katherine Philips and Lady Mary Wortley Montagu. Their explicit deprecations of publications are not to be trusted. The editors tell us that going into the archives, looking at the manuscripts – looking at what we are not expected to see – tells another story. All of our speakers have emphasized the pressures that were put on the women writers to change or suppress their written work. The advice may come from something as august as the Church or as tiresome as the Unidentified Reader, the 'UR,' the publisher's reader of whom Anne Wilkinson speaks. Wilkinson's UR follows another canon of criticism in criticizing the woman writer's work as gossipy, lightweight: 'there are too many letters.' Coldwell felt that Wilkinson's experience was recapitulated in her own run-in with her 'Reader B.' We all have a Reader B to try to satisfy.

The case is complicated by the extreme danger of knowledge of another person, knowledge sought by an editor. All of us here think of ourselves, I am sure, as Excellent Editors. We are, to borrow Barbara Pym's unnerving phrase, Excellent Women: conscientious, soundly scholarly, responsible. Yet every one of the Editing Women betrays some nervousness about her project, and a certain wariness about assuming that the editor's own arrangement of the material and the details would, can, ever might, or even should meet the desires, wishes, or needs of the defunct author. Coldwell uses the ultimate defence: that the author did not burn certain manuscript material (attempted autobiography, journals, drafts, letters) shows that she 'really' wanted it to be published. At the same time, we are all conscious of a fine line of trespass. The irony of the situation can hardly escape a woman editor, for men have so often assured us females that they [males] understand women's desires and needs better than women do themselves. This is a reflection of Rousseau's ferocious benevolence so famously expressed in *Emile*. Women must always be dishonest, says Rousseau, for 'nature' means it so. A man knows better what a woman means than she can say. But in the true inclinations of their nature, even in lying, they are not false at all: 'Why do you consult their mouth, when it is not that which ought to speak? Consult their eyes, their colouring, their breathing, their timid air, their soft resistance – there is the language which nature gives them in order to answer you.'[6]

Women won't say the truth about their desires. Beneath their evasive and inartificial fictionalizing of themselves, the skilled woman-reader (read 'rapist') can tell what she is truly after. Yes, there is an irony in the role of the female editor acting as the Rousseauean rapist-lover, with friendly violence snatching that which must be denied and yet would like to be taken. It is the editor who decides to include these sketches, these first drafts of manuscript, that hidden or forbidden work. It is indeed noticeable that all these editors editing the women want to – need to – go into the archives to look at the sacred, exciting, personal, handwritten, and unofficial material, in order to give it over to the public world. All the editors are conscious of this glorious trespass as somehow dubious and yet inevitable. The editor kisses up to her subject, but it is the Kiss of the Vampire.

I suppose this would be a good point at which to confess that I too have been a Vampire, and have not sworn off. My editing has been less adventurous, perhaps, than that of my fellow panelists. I have helped to produce for the world new editions of works by women writers, but I cannot claim to have introduced to the public notice any large or full text that was not there before. Neither have I destroyed the authenticity of any that have long been there. It depends, however, where the 'there' is. With Peter Sabor and Robert Mack I have produced for the public semi-popular reading editions, on a scholarly basis and fully annotated, of two of Frances Burney's novels, *Cecilia* and *The Wanderer*, in World's Classics from Oxford. I have also edited *sola* Burney's best-known novel, *Evelina*, for Penguin.[7] Editions of the novels and my biography of Burney seem intimately connected.[8] Hearing the speakers at this symposium, I am reminded over and over again that an editor is a kind of highly specialized biographer. Perhaps the editor is really a kind of primary biographer. In my case, what started out as a critical study of Burney's fiction went in two directions – to the editions of her works, for otherwise I couldn't find other readers with whom to discuss the books, and to the biography, so that I could myself engage in the fascinating if dangerous game of making sense of a life, stringing details together to form an artistically pleasing whole.

We are all conscious now, and were then, of the fictional nature of biography. We are now more conscious than ever of the fictional nature of the raw materials on which biographies rest – our primary sources. The journals and letters of the subject may be very artful constructions, rethinkings, persuasions, revisitings of memory, self-elaborations. That this is so has put the *art* of writing biography into some disrepute. When I started on Burney's, some people asked *why* I wanted to do it. I usually replied with the deliberately gross pragmatic answer, that I noticed that writers who had biographies written of them, even in this day and age, tended to be read more widely than those who didn't. So the biography, in a way, can be viewed as a pendant or a pointer to the works. It is likely to lead to more room being made on the library shelf for the writer. Biography also allows the inclusion of material for which the world is not yet ready, which may not be 'important' enough to find its way into any anthology and yet is still interesting.

Such, for me, was and is the set of verses written by Burney in May 1776 for her convalescent sister, 'To Sue on her recovery From the Jaundice.' This begins with a spring-songlike compliment to yellowness:

> When the Crocus & Snow-drop their *white* have display'd
> Come the Primrose & Cowslip, in *Yellow* array'd.

This is interesting, to me certainly. For one thing, it is one of the rare moments when Burney mentions flowers, and it exhibits an ironic sense of the tropes of floral loveliness, generally so suited to womankind and to female poets. The loved and lovely woman (Sister Sue) is connected to the erotic and delicate spring flowers through her jaundiced appearance. Illness, and what the world would think a real if temporary ugliness, are what make her floral. Traditions of erotic poetry and gallant convention seem to be good-humouredly shot at and shot up in this poem, which turns all the spring scene – including the other women, the 'Belles in the Street & the Park' in their yellow spring finery – into a reflection not through the jaundiced eye but of the jaundiced visage: 'And all like my Susan in *Jaundice* appear.' It gives us some hint that Burney took a good-naturedly jaundiced view of the floral clichés, and some idea of why she doesn't use them in her fiction, which is unusually flower-free.

Floral imagery was used against Burney, however, in her older years. In 1814 she produced her novel *The Wanderer*, which did not meet popular approval. After the victory over Napoleon, readers, or at least the critics of influential magazines, did not want to go again into the vexed questions of the early 1790s. John Wilson Croker, in his passionately unfavourable review of *The Wanderer* in the *Quarterly Review*, calls the author 'a mannerist who is *épuisée* [worn-out]':

> The Wanderer has the identical features of Evelina – but of Evelina grown old; the vivacity, the bloom, the elegance, the 'purple light of love' are vanished; the eyes are there, but they are dim; the cheek, but it is furrowed; the lips, but they are withered. And when to this description we add that Madame D'Arblay endeavours to make up for the want of originality in her characters by the most absurd mysteries ... and the most violent events, we have completed the portrait of an old coquette who endeavours, by the wild tawdriness and laborious gaiety of her attire, to compensate for the loss of the natural charms of freshness, novelty, and youth.[9]

Joan Coldwell says, in relation to Anne Wilkinson, that equating a woman's poetry with her pleasing appearance is dangerous, and of course destructive of anything like everlasting fame. When the body is gone, the poetry is gone too. Or when the woman has grown old, she can no longer 'please' in her writing, which is a 'natural' extension of her physical being. That what is wanted in women's writing is the 'purple light of love' seems as true in the age of Wilkinson as in the age of Burney. The devastating reviews of *The Wanderer* had their effect. Macaulay spoke ill of it in his magisterial review of all Burney's works, and even in the 1950s – but why should I say *even* – so ardent a Burney scholar as Joyce Hemlow agreed that there was no need to bring Burney's last novel in 'out of the shadows.'[10] Shadows best suit an aged beldame who has withered cheeks and whose tawdry finery should not be seen. If there is anything I am truly proud of in my editing, it is in having had the idea of bringing *The Wanderer* out. I know that its presence on the scene, with the appendices and notes, etc., has made a difference to the way in which Burney is viewed. At least with Burney I was not cumbered by a weight of social expectation, still less hindered by an immediate and interested posse of the author's relatives with a reputation to maintain. (Though there are Burney relatives extant, and some have joined our new organization, the Burney Society, which I invite you to join also.)

Working on Jane Austen has been an altogether different experience. I understand the guarded tones in which some of my fellow editors speak of the familial literary executors, the heirs of the family name, past and present. Jane Austen even has 'trustees,' at least according to an article in the *Daily Telegraph* about the latest spate of Austenian or Austen-related movies. The film *Clueless*, we were told, had given offence to Jane Austen's trustees. Who are Jane Austen's trustees? There is no such entity in legal existence, but one sees how natural it appears to assume such a body. Heirs and supporters have a share in Austen, or have taken shares in her, as if she were a cross between a corporation and a charity. Burney was nearly done in by being thought unimportant. Jane Austen is assaulted by the Heritage Concept, her image paralysed by what one might call the Heritage Nerve Gas. Austen is weighed down with propriety. It is, indeed, going into the manuscripts that tells us to what an extent this is so.

It was in investigating the supposedly minor questions of Jane Austen's supposedly very 'minor' verses that Douglas Murray and I encountered the Austen family tendency to rewrite and edit their Jane's *jeux d'esprit*. In the verse known by its first line as 'Maria, good-humoured, and handsome,' as it was first printed in the 1870 *Memoir* by James Edward Austen-Leigh, we have an edited version of a piece of work by Jane Austen which was first edited by James Edward's father, Austen's own brother James.[11] Jane Austen, in a letter of 1812, refers to this piece and the changes made in it: 'The 4 lines on Miss W. which I sent you were all my own, but James afterwards suggested what I thought a great improvement & as it stands in the Steventon Edition.'[12] The Steventon Edition appears to be a joking reference to the family-approved collection of family works. Perhaps Jane Austen is joking about the process of editorializing and officious changes that make her home *like* a publishing house.

A set of verses of more interest is Jane Austen's very last composition, written, or rather composed, three days before her death. We have entitled these 'When Winchester Races' (from the beginning of the first line), a work to which Chapman gave the pompous and Latinate title 'Venta.'[13] The version hitherto printed is based on a manuscript now at Chawton. The Chawton edition is smoother, more correct, 'improved' in James's way. The manuscript now in the Henry W. and Albert A. Berg Collection in the New York Public Library has been ruled out as a poor and erroneous scratch, but a look at it leads one to believe that this was actually the first version of the poem, written by Cassandra Austen to Jane Austen's dictation. The irregularities are of the kind that happen in taking dictation, particularly when the mind is distracted by something more important, like a great and lowering sorrow. Jane Austen died on 18 July 1817, and on 15 July she composed the comic verses about St. Swithin and the rained-out races. Jo Modert's valuable edition of *Jane Austen's Manuscript Letters* makes clear in the fine introduction that the younger generations of Austens cannot be trusted with the care or appreciation of Jane Austen's manuscripts.[14] In the Victorian era, the young Austens, now middle-aged and respectable, worried about letting anyone see 'When Winchester Races.' On her deathbed Jane Austen should have been thinking pious thoughts, not making up jokes.

Jane Austen's brother Henry had alluded to this last composition in the very first biographical piece about Austen, the 'Biographical Notice' written by him in 1817 and prefixed to the two novels published posthumously as one work, *Northanger Abbey* and *Persuasion*. But from 1833, before the Victorian Age had even got started, that reference was deleted from Henry's biographical notice. The first big biographical work on Austen was her nephew's *Memoir* in 1870. James Edward Austen-Leigh refused the request of the Earl of Stanhope to print in the second edition of the *Memoir* of his aunt the interesting verses that Stanhope had heard of but had never been able to read. The memoir-writer's sister, Jane Austen's niece Caroline, righteous daughter of brother James, voices her own disapproval in a letter expressing herself as vexed at 'Uncle Henry' for having mentioned the verses at all. Caroline certainly advised against publication of any kind. She was afraid that these lines would give the wrong impression: 'Introduced as the latest working of her mind ... the joke about the dead Saint, & the Winchester races all jumbled up together, would read badly as amongst the few details given of the closing scene.'[15] James Edward told the Earl the verses were 'too light and playful' to be included. Here indeed is a striking example of the power of heirs, executors, and publication gatekeepers. They can guard the Portrait of a Lady by keeping her works from the public eye. When the set of verses on Winchester was at length published, it appeared in the version that we believe to have been revised almost immediately by brother James, and not in the form in which it was dictated to Cassandra.

It seems an added irony that Jane Austen's own growing fame added to the desire to trim and trick out her biography and keep back some of her writing. Many of the artists we have looked at this weekend have suffered from pronounced lack of fame in certain centuries – Katherine Philips, Julian of Norwich, or even Lady Mary, who has lived in a half-light despite her famous *Turkish Letters*. Austen's fame grew and became established about fifty years after her death, and that was a point at which her relatives were most earnest in their desire to 'protect' her.

What executors execute is the will of some kind of social structure, or majority, or self-projection. If editors are fallible and to some extent deceitful, literary executors seem the Nightmare Life in Death to dear departed writers' writings – and I would add that the executor problem can burden male authors as well. T.S. Eliot comes to mind. Only, when a lady is in the case, the obfuscation always seems more justifiable. Her 'fame' is her 'good fame,' and a lady's reputation is better not handled at all. It is a matter for the shades.

A benevolent protection of her from her own inadequacies and mistakes seems such a worthy act – and I might point out that this posture of protection can be taken by other women. Note Caroline Austen's disdain for the comic verses and her concern that they would give the wrong impression of the 'closing scene,' which was not to her mind a satisfactory scene, there being too little material (or even too little detail of the right sort) to make out a large and satisfactory pious deathbed picture, which is evidently what she would have liked.

In this meeting we have throughout been speaking as if of course there are peculiar problems besetting women writers which are reflected not only in their fame or their dropping out of sight, but also in the very condition of their texts and the things that have happened before those texts come down to us, even in manuscript form. There are thus, it is argued, peculiar problems and interesting challenges presented to the women who edit these women, of which we can all speak and of which I have myself just spoken. Germaine Greer, in 'The Rewriting of Katherine Philips,' refers to the translated poems 'in the 1667 edition ... tidied up by the same smoothing hand.' Greer concludes that the poems of Katherine Philips have come down to us in heavily revised and very tricky versions, and that even the Rosania manuscript was 'probably less authoritative than supposed.' Greer warns that literary critics – especially including feminists – are too pleased with the revival of these women writers to ask what is appearing under their names.

> Feminist scholars who clamour for women's work to be included in the canon assume that there are texts attributed to women that actually represent what women wrote and the way they wrote it. The further back we go from our own time, the more unlikely that is.[16]

This is very true, and a most salutary warning. But one might paraphrase it thus: men who trumpet the value of the canon assume there are texts attributed to great male writers that actually represent what these men wrote and the way they wrote it. The further back we go from our own time, the more unlikely that is. Elsewhere, Greer says 'if we try to use the same procedures of bibliographical and textual investigation [as those recently used on Dickinson] on poets like Katherine Philips ... the texts that we have begin to fall apart in our hands.'[17] But I wish to stress that all texts tend to 'fall apart in your hands' as soon as you look at them.

It is *not* the case that we have simply splendid, solid, and indestructible texts of all male writers, and weak or inadequate and hopelessly lost texts of the women. One can fall in love with easeful death. One may even wish for the women, rather romantically, the condition of evanescence and transitory fragmentariness, a special state of butterfly-wing lost immortality. This can become just as sentimental as the desire for aerial fame, and as grossly repetitive as the desire for monuments more lasting than bronze and twice as brassy. The truth is that writing is a slippery business, and that the preservation of most 'texts,' as of most textiles, is due largely to sheer luck We would really not have known of Sophocles, apart from chance references elsewhere, save for *one* manuscript, which also preserves what we know of Aeschylus. Huge amounts of Greek drama were lost irrecoverably, including the bulk of the productions of Aeschylus, Sophocles, and Euripides. Chancy, chancy.

Virgil, on his deathbed, asked his friend and executor Varius to destroy the *Aeneid*, saying (truthfully) that it was not finished. Varius (and Maecenas) disregarded this plea and produced the *Aeneid*. But who knows how many changes they made in their friend's manuscript or what process of selection went on among various bits of paper or wax tablets, various workings of the same episode or description? We are not even sure how Virgil's poem actually begins: there are two versions of the beginning. Most scholars like to say that one was an earlier attempt and that the other is better, but that stylistic judgment rests on a tradition of editorial preference. With a poem so ancient and so *truly* irrecoverable, we have had to rest content, and will have to rest content, with the executor's and editor's production of a 'text' as if it were solid. But on reading the *Aeneid* you can see where the rents, holes, and incompleteness show through – it is like a fabric never completely mended.

And what of England's boast, her great and greatly canonized Shakespeare? We all know how the variants have been picked over to make unified and unitary texts of each play. Now that process itself has been much questioned. The 'Solid State Text' as we know it is arguably a nineteenth-century invention, resting on certain principles adopted in the Renaissance and solidified in the Enlightenment. But that Solid State Text may be going out all over Europe. Unified monoliths are somewhat out of fashion at the moment, a trend which has its political aspects, and some implications not altogether good for a unified Canada too. A former colleague of Professor Coldwell and myself, Michael Warren, has been very active in arguing that *King Lear* is not a single work begging to be made into one through rearrangement of its various fragments and altered states, but on the contrary that it is at least *two* different plays, two versions of the same motif, written by Shakespeare at different times.[18] So here is a major canonical work by a Dead White Male which is hopelessly hard to ascertain, a work whose status is up in the air, or up for grabs, or up the spout.

Of course I could go on and on reciting other examples of textual problems. The whole of the eighteenth century is a vast set of textual problems. As I found in working on *The Daring Muse*, a poem by any poet when you start looking at it 'falls to pieces in your hands,' as Greer would say.[19] William Shenstone's 'The Schoolmistress,' a popular poem but by no means claimed as a major effort, seems to exist in a different version every time it is set out in print. How to set Gray's 'Elegy' properly on the page is a question in itself. The edition we have of Pope is scandalously outdated and claims a false authority. *The Dunciad* at the very least needs to be tackled all over again. And one of my favourite authors, Samuel Richardson, published his great novel *Clarissa* in so many variant versions (not to speak of the manuscript copies which we know were in circulation) that a Variorum edition would be fascinating but impossible fully to produce save electronically.

The editing of the future will not only use computers in getting up a text and in writing introductions, indices, etc., but will also leave its best and most fluent product on the database. The ultimate 'best' edition will not be in hard copy but in a computer version, with all the variants and almost infinite notes which the reader will be able to access at will. Thus a reader perusing a single or hard-copy version will know that this is not the whole story, and on a given day this scholarly reader may decide to tackle one particular lyric, or canto 11, or volume 2, letter 14, or whatever, by turning to the database and seeing the variants. Branching off from this will be other raw material – notes, journals, letters, etc., as well as other editors' and critics' comments. I think any one of the women authors discussed at this conference would fare better on a CD-ROM version, where a nearly simultaneous representation of material is possible. The increasing presence and presentedness of such richly various versions will render the notion of the established or 'definitive' text laughable. The reader can make his or her own 'text' on Tuesday and can make a different one on Wednesday. The writer's questions, the hesitations, the processes of mind would then have a new place – a new kind of place – and reader and editor would move closer together. Indeed, reader would become editor or secondary editor, putting together in new combinations the materials that a primary editor would offer.

I have been very glad to have this stimulating chance to think about editing and its puzzles and problems – the sharp questions that are posed. I do wonder, just a little, to what extent it is right to cut a discussion of Editing Women off from a discussion of Editing Men.

Should we really treat the matter as altogether separate? Isn't that attributing a kind of false invincibility to male authors and editors? I am a feminist, and proud to declare myself such, even in an era not particularly favourable to that appellation. But I don't want to create a heavy fence between 'male editing' and 'female editing.' I have worked with people of the 'opposite' gender in editing Richardson, a male author, and I have got men to join me in editing Burney and Austen, female authors. I am quite proud of having roped in Peter Sabor when I was faced with editing Burney's *Cecilia*. This was the beginning of important developments. We went on to edit *The Wanderer* together, and Peter was so inspired by the experience that he became a Burney expert of considerable power, and has since gone on to the difficult and fascinating job of editing all of Burney's manuscript plays.[20] It may be my prejudice, but in editorial projects I like working with other people. But I do want to think of the enterprise always as ultimately a joint one, and as an enterprise always and perpetually under review.

I think the involvement of women in editing women (as well as men) can be productive of highly important new insights. I see scholarly women as bringing to our endeavour some new viewpoints and some fascinatingly different expectations. These Editing Women possess, at least at this particular time at the end of the twentieth century, the advantage of not being much swayed by older notions of 'proper' editing. They are eager to descend into the jumble, to the tangled archival skein, and less inspired to rush to decisive knot-cutting than editors (male or female) brought up on the traditional view of what an edition is. Feminist criticism of a number of kinds has created different perspectives, so that what is 'important' is identified very differently. I see these insights and the practices they give rise to as likely to affect all future editors, male or female.

Indeed, the essentialism we are talking in is very largely a product of cultural history, and I see no reason to believe that men and women must be hunting different Snarks forever and a day. Isobel Grundy speaks of the title *The Complete Letters* as one she would not now use. I am glad she voiced her sense of that change. Among the rising generation around us just entering graduate school, Grundy's present and converted view of the suspect nature of the' authoritative edition,' the fallacy of the 'complete' anything, would be widely shared, even perhaps taken for granted. We too are affected by the *Zeitgeist*, though I will not go so far as to say creatures of it. In a long life in academe I have been affected by historical currents touching us all, so that what

I want or have been taught to expect of a text now is truly different from what I wanted or was taught to want at the beginning of my career. My own preferences run against overediting. They go against, for instance, the modernization of the expressive Enlightenment page, so that I regard the *Yale Johnson*, say, with condescending detestation.[21] It is my turn to crow, to say, 'Oh, they started out with the wrong principles.' But neither principles nor editors were 'wrong,' only right by the standards of a period just gone and not my own.

I hope and believe that we will keep on writing and editing and talking about texts, and our own difficulties with texts, and the fragile, funny work of 'creating a text.' Because the women writers have been left out so much, or jammed into shapes that didn't fit them, there is room to talk about them separately. And there is room too to give vent to our own feelings of relatedness or anxiety in dealing with these women writers and the proliferation around them of what is not official clean 'text' or magisterial 'work.'

I think this symposium could provide inspiration for all sorts of editors. We are making a little news here in Toronto, hearing the News about editing. It is always exciting to hear some new news. The pride we feel is not unlike that of the old Renaissance humanists, who boasted about releasing works from manuscript, from a tenuous and shadowy existence, and raising them into the safety of print. Editors rescue texts. As the editor of the first printed edition of Heliodorus says of his manuscript of the *Aethiopica*, the book itself ought to be grateful to its patrons:

> If by you he is in a manner born again, just as if he were brought
> back from the underworld, that is from the beetles and larvae, from
> prison and darkness, from mould and neglectful filth, and from
> threatened annihilation.[22]

How we rejoice, we editors, that we liberate our works into the light, get them away from the beetles and larvae, the dismal and uncertain state. This can be done only by first pointing out what a tenuous state they are in at present. We all want to liberate our authors into the light. That 'liberation' may be a psychodrama in which we liberate ourselves – doubtless it is – but that should not spoil our pleasure in saying 'Look! There is more!' or 'Look! There's more to it!' We shall be saying both these things as we go in, even while asserting that *women's* writing is always fragile, perhaps romantically doomed to a perpetual evanescence and a dying of the light. *All* writing is fragile and evanescent. Think of all the 'great works' that we haven't heard of – and cannot even lament! The survival of any work of written art is a kind of triumph, and should be cause for perpetual astonishment, and some cheer.

NOTES

1 *Kissing the Rod: An Anthology of Seventeenth-Century Women's Verse*, ed. Germaine Greer et al. (London: Virago, 1988).

2 Germaine Greer, *Slip-Shod Sibyls: Recognition, Rejection, and the Woman Poet* (London: Viking, 1995).

3 Riddy, above p. 106.

4 Riddy, above p. 104.

5 Coldwell, above p. 7.

6 Jean-Jacques Rousseau, *Emile, ou de l'éducation*, ed. Michael Launay (Paris: Garnier Flammarion, 1966), 505: 'Pourquoi consultez-vouz leur bouche, quand ce n'est pas elle qui doit parler? Consultez leurs yeux, leur teint, leur respiration, leur air craintif, leur molle résistance: voilà le langage que la nature leur donne pour vouz répondre' (my translation).

7 Frances Burney, *The Wanderer*, ed. Margaret Anne Doody, Robert L. Mack, and Peter Sabor (Oxford: Oxford University Press, 1991); Burney, *Cecilia*, ed. Peter Sabor and Margaret Anne Doody (Oxford: Oxford University Press, 1988); Burney, *Evelina*, ed. Margaret Anne Doody (Harmondsworth: Penguin, 1994).

8 Margaret Anne Doody, *Frances Burney: The Life and the Works* (New Brunswick, NJ: Rutgers University Press, 1988).

9 Unsigned review of *The Wanderer* by John Wilson Croker, *Quarterly Review* 11 (April 1814): 124–6, quoted in Doody, *Frances Burney*, 385.

10 Thomas Babington Macaulay, *Edinburgh Review* 76 (January 1843): 545; Joyce Hemlow, *The History of Fanny Burney* (Oxford: Clarendon Press, 1958), 338–9.

11 James Edward Austen-Leigh, *A Memoir of Jane Austen by her Nephew* (London: Bentley, 1870), 88.

12 The manuscript of this letter written by Jane Austen on 29 November 1812 is now in the Henry W. and Albert A. Berg Collection in the New York Public Library (Astor, Lenox, and Tilden Foundations). See also Jane Austen, *Catharine and Other Writings*, ed. Margaret Anne Doody and Douglas Murray (Oxford: Oxford University Press, 1993), 244, 280–1.

13 Jane Austen, *Minor Works*, ed. R.W. Chapman (Oxford: Oxford University Press, 1969), 451–2.

14 Jane Austen, *Jane Austen's Manuscript Letters in Facsimile*, ed. Jo Modert (Carbondale: Southern Illinois University Press, 1990), xix–xxix.

15 Letter of Caroline Austen to her brother James Edward Austen-Leigh, July 1871, quoted in Austen, *Manuscript Letters*, xxiii–xxiv. See also Deirdre Le Faye, 'Jane Austen's Verses and Lord Stanhope's Disappointment,' *The Book Collector* 37 (1988): 86–91.

16 Greer, *Slip-Shod Sibyls*, 171–2.

17 Greer, *Slip-Shod Sibyls*, xvii.

18 See for example *The Division of the Kingdoms: Shakespeare's Two Versions of 'King Lear,'* ed. Gary Taylor and Michael Warren (Oxford: Clarendon Press, 1983).

19 Margaret Anne Doody, *The Daring Muse: Augustan Poetry Reconsidered* (Cambridge: Cambridge University Press, 1985).

20 Frances Burney, *The Complete Plays*, ed. Peter Sabor (London: W. Pickering, 1995).

21 *The Yale Edition of the Works of Samuel Johnson*, 15 volumes (New Haven: Yale University Press, 1958–85).

22 Vincentus Opsopaeus, *Heliodorou Aithiopikes Historias Biblia Deka* (Basel: Hervagiana, 1534), a2r–a2v: 'si per uos quodammodo renatus, & tanquam ab inferis reductus, hoc est à blattis & tineis, à carcere & tenebris, à situ squalore, & interitu, cui proximus erat, liberatus in lucem emerserit' (my translation).

MEMBERS OF THE CONFERENCE

Nike Abbot, Canadian Broadcasting Corporation
Mary Arseneau, University of Ottawa
Elaine Averbach, Wilfrid Laurier University
Mary Baldwin, University of Toronto Press
Dunja Baus, University of Toronto
Frances Beer, York University
Elizabeth Bentley, self-employed
Gerald Bentley, University of Toronto
Naomi Black, York University
Jan Blathwayt, York University
Karen Boersma, University of Toronto Press
Paula Bourner, Brock University
Martha Bowden, Kennesaw State College
Maria Broser, Wilfrid Laurier University
Heather Campbell, York University
James Carley, York University/University of Cambridge
Lynda Chiotti, Editors' Association of Canada
Lorna Clark, Ottawa
Cherry Clayton, University of Guelph
Joan Coldwell, McMaster University
Viviana Comensoli, Wilfrid Laurier University
Brian Corman, University of Toronto
Jane Couchman, York University
Sherrill Credo, Government of Ontario
Tara Curtis, University of Guelph
Judith Deitch, University of Toronto
Penelope Reed Doob, York University
Margaret Anne Doody, Vanderbilt University
Ann Dooley, University of Toronto
Donna Duncan, Wilfrid Laurier University
JoAnna Dutka, University of Toronto
Len Early, York University
Mary Ebos, York University
Charmaine Eddy, Trent University
Joanne Findon, York University/University of Toronto
Patricia Fleming, University of Toronto
Jennifer Forbes, University of Toronto
Roberta Frank, University of Toronto
David Galbraith, University of Toronto
Anne Galler, Concordia University

Susan Glover, University of Toronto
Walter Goffart, University of Toronto
Susanne Goodison, Queen's University
Ann-Barbara Graff, University of Toronto
John Grant, University of Toronto
Germaine Greer, University of Cambridge
Claire Grogan, Bishop's University
Isobel Grundy, University of Alberta
Sandra Hagan, McMaster University
Edna Hajnal, University of Toronto
Francess Halpenny, University of Toronto
Lesley Higgins, York University
Lara Hinchberger, University of Toronto
S. Howson, University of Toronto
Linda Hutcheon, University of Toronto
Ann Hutchison, University of Toronto
Dean Irvine, University of Calgary
Heather Jackson, University of Toronto
Janelle Jenstad, Queen's University
Nancy Johnston, York University
Miriam Jones, York University
Beverly Kennedy, Marianopolis College
Lorna Knight, National Library of Canada
Marie Korey, University of Toronto
Richard Landon, University of Toronto
Nicole Langlois
Chantel Lavoie, University of Toronto
Paula Leverage, University of Toronto
Verna Linney, York University
Rota Lister, University of Waterloo
Evelyn Mackie, University of Toronto
Lorna Marsden, Wilfrid Laurier University
Linda Marshall, University of Guelph
B. Martin, York University
Katherine Martyn, University of Toronto
Jeremy Maule, University of Cambridge
Fiona MacCool, York University
Barbara McLean, University of Western Ontario
Randall McLeod, University of Toronto
Laura McRae, University of Toronto
Marietta Messmer, York University

Liz Millward, York University
Carol Mitchell, Concordia University
Raimonda Modiano, University of Washington
Heather Murray, University of Toronto
Meghan Nieman, University of Toronto
Tracey Ormerod, York University
Elsie Paget, McMaster University
Cynthia Park, University of Toronto
John Parsons, University of Toronto
Joyce Parsons, University of Guelph
Anne Pilgrim, York University
Heljé Porré, York University
Suzanne Rancourt, University of Toronto Press
Margaret Reeves, University of Toronto
Felicity Riddy, University of York
Janet Ritch, Université de Paris/Sorbonne
S.P. Rosenbaum, University of Toronto
Erika Rummel, Wilfrid Laurier University
Anne Russell, Wilfrid Laurier University
Ann Saddlemyer, University of Toronto
Rose Sheinin, University of Toronto
Ann Shteir, York University
Marie-France Silver, York University
Clara Thomas, York University
Eleanor Ty, Wilfrid Laurier University
Fred Unwalla, University of Toronto
Tatiana Usachev, University of Toronto
Nina Van Gessel, McMaster University
Germaine Warkentin, University of Toronto
Nicholas Watson, University of Western Ontario
Stephanie Wells, University of Toronto Press
Bonnie Wheeler, Southern Methodist University
Joan Winearls, University of Toronto
Jeanne Wood, York University
Susanne Woods, Brown University

PREVIOUS CONFERENCE PUBLICATIONS

1965 *Editing Sixteenth-Century Texts*, ed. R.J. Schoeck (1966)
1966 *Editing Nineteenth-Century Texts*, ed. John M. Robson (1967)
1967 *Editing Eighteenth-Century Texts*, ed. D.I.B. Smith (1968)
1968 *Editor, Author, and Publisher*, ed. Wm. J. Howard (1969)
1969 *Editing Twentieth-Century Texts*, ed. Francess G. Halpenny (1972)
1970 *Editing Seventeenth-Century Prose*, ed. D.I.B. Smith (1972)
1971 *Editing Poetry from Spenser to Dryden*, ed. John M. Baird (1972)
1972 *Editing Canadian Texts*, ed. Francess G. Halpenny (1975)
1973 *Editing Eighteenth-Century Novels*, ed. G.E. Bentley (1975)
1974 *Editing British and American Literature, 1880–1920*, ed. Eric W. Domville (1976)
1975 *Editing Renaissance Dramatic Texts*, ed. Anne Lancashire (1976)
1976 *Editing Medieval Texts*, ed. A.G. Rigg (1977)
1977 *Editing Nineteenth-Century Fiction*, ed. Jane Millgate (1978)
1978 *Editing Correspondence*, ed. J.A. Dainard (1979)
1979 *Editing Illustrated Books*, ed. William Blissett (1980)
1980 *Editing Poetry from Spenser to Dryden*, ed. A.D. deQuehen (1981)
1981 *Editing Texts in the History of Science and Medicine*, ed. Trevor H. Levere (1982)
1982 *Editing Polymaths*, ed. H.J. Jackson (1983)
1983 *Editing Early English Drama*, ed. A.F. Johnston (1987)
1984 *Editing, Publishing, and Computer Technology*, ed. Sharon Butler and William P. Stoneman (1988)
1985 *Editing and Editors*, ed. Richard Landon (1988)
1986 *Editing Modern Economists*, ed. D.E. Moggridge (1988)
1987 *Editing Greek and Latin Texts*, ed. John N. Grant (1989)
1988 *Crisis in Editing: Texts of the English Renaissance*, ed. Randall McLeod (1994)
1989 *Challenges, Projects, Texts: Canadian Editing*, ed. John Lennox and Janet M. Paterson (1993)
1990 *Music Discourse from Classical to Early Modern Times*, ed. Rika Maniates (1997)
1991 *The Politics of Editing Medieval Texts*, ed. Roberta Frank (1992)
1992 *Critical Issues in Editing Exploration Texts*, ed. Germaine Warkentin (1995)
1993 *Editing Early and Historical Atlases*, ed. Joan Winearls (1995)
1994 *Editing Texts from the Age of Erasmus*, ed. Erika Rummel (1996)
1995 *Editing Women*, ed. Ann M. Hutchison (1998)